Llewellyn's
2016
Witches'
Companion

An Almanac for Everyday Living

Llewellyn's 2016 Witches' Companion

ISBN 978-0-7387-3401-9

Art Director: Lynne Menturweck
Cover art © Tim Foley
Cover designer: Lynne Menturweck
Designer: Joanna Willis
Editor: Andrea Neff

Interior illustrations:
Kathleen Edwards: 18, 22, 82, 85, 86, 109, 113, 134, 139, 191, 195, 196, 253, 259
Tim Foley: 9, 27, 30, 73, 77, 79, 123, 127, 130, 143, 182, 184, 187, 209, 242, 247, 248
Bri Hermanson: 33, 36, 39, 89, 93, 201, 202, 205, 263, 265, 268
Jennifer Hewitson: 11, 14, 64, 68, 70, 119, 120, 145, 149, 150, 172, 175, 179, 234, 236, 238
Christa Marquez: 43, 44, 47, 50, 97, 99, 101, 105, 153, 155, 156, 160, 213, 215, 217
Rik Olson: 53, 57, 60, 164, 166, 169, 221, 223, 227, 230

Additional illustrations: Llewellyn Art Department

Any Internet references contained in this work are current at publication time, but the publisher cannot guarantee that a specific location will continue to be maintained.

You can order Llewellyn annuals and books from *New Worlds*, Llewellyn's magazine catalog. To request a free copy of the catalog, call toll-free 1-877-NEW-WRLD or visit our website at http://www.llewellyn.com.

Llewellyn Worldwide Ltd.
2143 Wooddale Drive
Woodbury, MN 55125-2989
www.llewellyn.com

Printed in the United States of America

Contents

Community Forum

Provocative Opinions on Contemporary Topics

TESS WHITEHURST

Why "Fluffy Bunny" Isn't Funny • 10

As someone who calls on angels and generally incorporates a lot of New Age–inspired thought into her magical practice, Tess Whitehurst is not fond of the term "fluffy bunny." In this article, she discusses a number of reasons why it is unfair to disparagingly slap this label onto other Witches—and what you can say instead.

JAMES KAMBOS

To Walk a New Path • 17

Are you at a crossroads, ready to walk a new spiritual path, but you don't know how or where to start? James Kambos offers helpful tips based on his own journey back to the Old Religion.

BARBARA ARDINGER

Practical Lessons in Kindness and Gratitude
from the Grasshopper and the Ant • 25

In this humorous retelling of a fable by Jean de La Fontaine, Barbara Ardinger presents a timeless lesson in kindness and gratitude.

BOUDICA FOSTER

Leaving a Legacy in the Pagan Community · 32

*With the recent passing of some wonderful elders in the Pagan community,
Boudica Foster got to wondering: What ideas or concepts can we leave behind
to help foster successful community in the next generation of Pagans?*

LINDA RAEDISCH

A Place in the Sun: The Lur of the Nordic Bronze Age · 42

*Most of Germanic Paganism is drawn from the Iron Age, but there's much
inspiration to be found in Scandinavia's Bronze Age. Linda Raedisch takes
you on a tour of the Nordic Bronze Age, where you'll witness ancient Paganism
in action!*

MONICA CROSSON

Pagan Standard Time (PST): A Tale for Tolerance · 52

*When Monica Crosson mistakenly brings her Evangelical Christian sister to
a Pagan gathering, she hopes her sister will have so much fun that she won't
notice. That works fine until a young man dressed as Pan holds up his drinking
horn and exclaims, "We're on Pagan Standard Time!" In the end, both woman
learn valuable lessons in tolerance and understanding.*

JYMI X/Ø ("REVEREND VARIABLE")

Discordianism: A Taste of April Foolery All Year Round · 63

*For Jymi x/ø, Discordianism is about keeping things moving and changing.
It's about recognizing the need for both order and chaos. If you wish to explore
a Discordian path, be prepared to make it up yourself—all of it.*

STEPHANIE WOODFIELD

The Path of a Priestess · 72

*What exactly is a priestess? There is a tendency in the Pagan community to
consider anyone who leads a ritual or coven to be a priest or priestess. But
for Stephanie Woodfield, the defining function of a priestess is to serve as an
intermediary between the gods and the community.*

Witchy Living

Day-by-Day Witchcraft

CASSIUS SPARROW

What to Do When Your Magick Doesn't Work • 80

We all go through times when it seems like our spells and petitions simply aren't working. Cassius Sparrow offers practical advice to get a Witch up out of a funk and back into the magick.

LAUREL REUFNER

We Are Everywhere: Finding Pagans in the Wild • 88

Encountering fellow Pagans in everyday life can be challenging but is also rewarding. Laurel Reufner teaches you what to look for—and how to make yourself visible to others in the know.

SUSAN PESZNECKER

Why Is Journaling Such an Angsty Process
for So Many People? • 95

Journaling can be incredibly valuable if you work with spiritual paths, deities, tools, natural forces, or other magickal mojo. Susan Pesznecker demystifies the process and covers everything you need to know to develop a rewarding, soul-enriching, joyful practice.

NAJAH LIGHTFOOT

Spiritual Cleansing at the Crossroads • 108

As Witches, we perform many works for others, but taking care of ourselves often seems to fall to the bottom of the list—leaving our empathetic and intuitive senses muddled and unclear. A cleansing at the crossroads can be just what we need to clear the spiritual air and step onto a new path.

BARBARA ARDINGER

Adding Mindfulness to Our Lives • 116

Let's be present in our lives, and let's be grateful for our blessings and pay them forward. Barbara Ardinger explores the benefits of mindfulness and provides exercises to help you pay more attention to your life.

EMBER GRANT

Spice Up Your Magic · 122

Most modern Witches use herbs in their everyday lives, but how many venture into the realm of spices, except when cooking? Ember Grant investigates five inexpensive and easy-to-obtain spices and their magical applications.

AUTUMN DAMIANA

The Magical and Spiritual Uses of Diet · 132

Autumn Damiana examines different types of diets that are commonly followed by magical folk (vegan/vegetarian, no-salt, organic, raw food, ancestral, cleanse, Paleo, etc.) and highlights the pros and cons of each.

Witchcraft Essentials

Practices, Rituals & Spells

JANE MEREDITH

Magical Kids · 144

Doing magic with kids can be fun, simple, and effective. Jane Meredith presents three magic spells to work with children: a gingerbread spell to change reality, a spell to counter nightmares, and a healing spell.

MICHAEL FURIE

From Shadows to Light:
An Overview of Banishing and Polarization · 152

Banishing and polarization are two techniques used by Witches to rid the environment of negativity. In this article, Michael Furie addresses the positive points and and potential pitfalls of both methods and when to use them.

BLAKE OCTAVIAN BLAIR

Easy Guide to Guided Meditations · 161

Guided meditation is an effective method for grounding, relaxation, meeting spirit guides, and a variety of other purposes. Blake Octavian Blair offers his perspective on how to create simple guided meditations of your own, as well as tips for customizing your meditations for a few common specific purposes.

CHARLIE RAINBOW WOLF

Smudge Plants and How to Use Them • 171

A smudging ceremony has many purposes, from purging energies to connecting to all four elements. Charlie Rainbow Wolf takes a look at what plants and herbs can be included in a smudge ceremony, and how to cultivate and dry them.

LEXA OLICK

Written in Stone: An Ancient Tool in a Modern World • 181

The use of stones is a traditional part of modern-day Witchcraft, but discover how even seemingly ordinary routines evolved from ancient practices. Then make your own beaded stone, which can be a tribute to a past memory, a small icon to honor nature, or even a gift.

EMYME

Magickal Monikers • 189

Your magickal name is out in the universe waiting for you to claim it. Without you realizing or knowing it, clues and hints have been set before you all of your life. Use the techniques in this article to create your own magickal moniker.

ESTHAMARELDA MCNEVIN

Recognizing and Combating the Evil Eye:
Putting It On and Poking It Out • 199

Esthamarelda McNevin examines the predatory use of an age-old sympathetic charm and the trusted methods commonly employed to combat anti-social magic.

Magical Transformations

Everything Old Is New Again

MELANIE MARQUIS

Big Magick for a Small World • 210

Today's magickal practitioners often reserve their charms solely for the purpose of achieving goals of personal development—but there's a whole world out there that needs your help! Melanie Marquis discusses techniques you can use to make your globally minded spellwork both easier and more effective.

NATALIE ZAMAN

Tower of Truth, Wall of Wonder:
A Ritual to Heal a Painful Past • 220

If you bear scars from your childhood, it may be time to do some serious repair work. Natalie Zaman shares healing techniques to help overcome a painful past.

TIFFANY LAZIC

Leaping from Zeus's Head: How Athena
Helps Combat Negative Thinking • 232

There is wisdom to be gleaned from the painful thoughts in our heads. Athena offers us powerful tools that can help us release our concerns and find peace.

KRISTOFFER HUGHES

Cerridwen: Meeting the Witch Goddess • 240

Learn how to deepen your connection to Cerridwen, and allow her message of wisdom, enchantment, and magic to filter through your dreams and inspire your waking life.

DIANA RAJCHEL

The Divine Masculine for Women • 251

Discover how to approach the God on new, healthy, non-patriarchal terms, and how to create a meaningful role for the divine masculine in your own practice.

ELIZABETH BARRETTE

The Inward Bridge: Massage and
the Mind-Body Connection • 262

Elizabeth Barrette explains some basic ideas about the mental and physical aspects of bodywork, and how it helps unite the mind and the body.

The Lunar Calendar

September 2015 to December 2016

CALENDAR WITH HOLIDAYS AND NEW & FULL MOONS • 271

Community Forum

PROVOCATIVE OPINIONS ON
CONTEMPORARY TOPICS

Why "Fluffy Bunny" Isn't Funny

Tess Whitehurst

You may have noticed that a certain faction of the Pagan community has succeeded in coining a religious slur for people who are ostensibly within their own group. And in case you don't quite see it that way, it's my intention to convince you that "fluffy bunny" *is*, in fact, a religious slur.

The first time I encountered the term was by way of a Facebook post that was going around. I don't remember what it said (something about how to tell the difference between a fluffy bunny and a *real* Witch), but right away I recognized myself as someone who was very likely to be called such a thing behind my back.

After all, I like rainbows and angels. I like positive affirmations. I like to be inclusive of diverse spiritual practices and beliefs. I don't eat meat or animal products because I do my best not to hurt or harm any living thing. I try to avoid affecting others' free

will or sending out negativity, because I believe that what I send out comes back in some form. In short, my witchy palette is tinged with lightness, brightness, and decidedly New Agey sensibilities.

I wasn't thrilled to learn that there was a disparaging nickname for people like me. To be frank, it hurt my feelings. Before I saw the Facebook post, I hadn't any inkling that mentioning white light might cause someone in such a seemingly open-minded community to utter a derogatory snicker. After I saw the post, I felt a spiritual self-consciousness at Pagan gatherings that I never thought I'd feel.

If you think about it, the whole thing isn't actually that surprising. Remember in junior high and high school how the people who were most likely to call someone names were actually the most wounded deep down? *They* were tired of a lifetime of living in fear of rejection and ridicule, so they rejected and ridiculed others in an effort to beat everyone to the punch. Considering that, in general, Pagans are often considered the weirdos and outcasts in our predominantly monotheistic culture, it follows that some Pagans would seek out a way to reject a subset of their own counterculture. It confers a sense of power and superiority by allowing *them* (for once!) to be the one ridiculing someone else's path.

Now, some of you may be feeling defensive at this point. After all, you didn't *think* you were being mean or throwing around religious slurs! You just thought "fluffy bunny" was a cute little inside joke. Well, first of all, definitely don't beat yourself up! We're all always learning and changing and growing, and every single person makes mistakes. And second, just in case you're still not convinced that fluffy bunny is an unkind and unnecessary moniker, let me present the following arguments.

Calling Someone a Name Is Always Hurtful

"Fluffy bunny" doesn't *sound* like a terrible name, but it *is* insulting—because you know that when you're called that, or even when you think you may be called that behind your back, it's clearly intended as a dismissal and diminishment of your importance as a Witch and as a human. Just as calling a woman a seemingly benign name such as "airhead" or "dingbat" is actually a chauvinistic move meant to diminish her perceived authority, "fluffy bunny" is used to convince the listener that the person they deem deserving of that name is not to be taken seriously.

> **"Fluffy bunny" doesn't *sound* like a terrible name, but it *is* insulting—because you know that when you're called that, or even when you think you may be called that behind your back, it's clearly intended as a dismissal and diminishment of your importance as a Witch and as a human.**

Labeling Someone Makes It Difficult to Respect or Learn from Them

The minute you label someone, you cut yourself off from experiencing the fullness of who that person is. Personally, I find that I learn the most and feel the most alive when I think of everyone as a teacher, and as everyone being inherently worthy of my respect and attention. Although, like everyone, my ego sometimes takes over and I find myself playing the imaginary "who is better than who" game, my true self knows that we are all equal and we are all equally valuable, even if our talents and strengths appear in different ways. Indeed, those differences are what make life interesting and what allow us to learn from each other. Labeling other types of people—especially with labels that are intended to be dismissive—insulates us from the great learning potential that comes from a celebration of diversity.

You Don't Really Know What Another Person's Spiritual Path Entails

So someone strikes you as preferring her Witchcraft with a larger helping of white light and rose petals than you do. Do you really *know* what her spiritual path entails? Yes, she may have mentioned misting her home with "airy-fairy sparkle spray," but how do you know that she doesn't also study the Eleusinian mysteries, or obscure translations of the *I Ching*, or some other weighty spiritual topic? Or maybe when she really needs to, she can exorcise even the most stubborn entities or perform an invisibility spell that would blow you away! She may seem fluffy on the surface, but the truth is, you really don't know, do you? Assuming you do know and then slapping her with the "fluffy bunny" label would be judging before you really know what you're judging. You know another word for pre-judging someone? Prejudice.

It's Not Really Your Business Anyway

It's not really your job to be the Witch police anyway, is it? Who ever said that we needed a running commentary on which practices are in and which are out, or on who is serious enough about the Craft and who isn't? Really, even if you *did* know what another Witch did in her most private spiritual moments, why would you feel the need to judge whether this was worthy of your approval? Everyone is different, and spirituality is highly personal. Just because something doesn't work for you doesn't mean it's not going to work for someone else.

Spiritual Shaming Contributes to a Culture of Shame

Do we really want to be part of a community that habitually shuns and shames its own? For example, I genuinely love calling on the popular New Age ascended master Saint Germain to transmute negativity with his violet flame. Personally, I find that it brings great joy to my heart and leaves quite a beautiful energetic effect in its wake. If I find myself surrounded by people who use terminology (such as "fluffy bunny") that seeks to instill shame in me for that, I will do one of three things. I will (a) do what I am doing now and consciously educate others about why it's not appropriate to do such a thing, (b) ignore the people saying such things and perhaps move on to a different spiritual community, or (c) believe them and begin to feel shame around following the natural path of my spirit. Let's hope that those of us who feel this way go with option A. This way, we can continue to benefit from the things that make our community great: our open-mindedness, our emphasis on personal power and self-love, our inclusion of various techniques and modalities, and our enthusiasm about learning from each other and from our differences.

What to Say Instead

Now, I understand that sometimes you might legitimately want words to describe something for which you previously would have used the term "fluffy bunny." For example, perhaps you want to tell a friend why you don't want to attend a certain lecture. Instead of saying, "The teacher is too much of a fluffy bunny for me," I suggest that you say something more along the lines of, "I don't resonate with that teacher's material because it's more New Agey than I prefer." That way, it's not about why you don't think the teacher is a legitimate Witch, it's about why the teachings don't match your current enthusiasms. It's less personal. Similarly, instead of saying, "That author is such a fluffy bunny," you might say, "Her books aren't really my style, because I prefer less eclectic material." Statements like these would be far less judgmental while communicating that just because someone doesn't share your personal tastes, it doesn't mean you believe that the person is not worthy of respect.

Let Go of *Om*-ophobia

When it comes right down to it, we all have a balance of light and dark aspects: when expressed in healthy ways, neither is inherently better or worse than the other, and we will probably naturally sway within the spectrum throughout our magical lives. When we criticize others, it's often because there's something about them that we're not willing to embrace within ourselves. If, in the past, you've felt the need to use the term "fluffy bunny," perhaps it's simply an indication that there is a part of you that's craving expression. Could it be that there's a sunshiny, chant-happy, harp-music-loving part of you that's aching to be embraced? Just in case the answer is yes, maybe it's time to try something new. Let me suggest that you let go of your *om*-ophobia and let your lighter, brighter, New Agier side out to play. Don't worry: you can always go back to your old ways, and the Witch police won't come haul you away.

And whether or not you uncover a latent interest in sparkles and rainbows, you're sure to find that it just feels better to speak kindly of others and to be respectful of the full spectrum of Pagan spiritual expression.

Tess Whitehurst *is an award-winning author, feng shui consultant, and intuitive counselor who presents ancient, sacred, and highly empowering wisdom in an extremely friendly and accessible way. She's written six books that have been translated into nine languages, and her articles have appeared in such places as* Writer's Digest, Whole Life Times, *and* Law of Attraction *magazine. She's appeared on morning news shows on both Fox and NBC, and her feng shui work was featured on the Bravo TV show* Flipping Out. *Tess lives with her longtime boyfriend, Ted Bruner, and their magical black cat, Solo, in a cozy, incense-scented, twinkle-light-lit country house near Columbia, MO. Visit her at www.tesswhitehurst.com.*

Illustrator: Jennifer Hewitson

To Walk a New Path

James Kambos

As I write this, I'm thinking of a letter I received years ago from a Llewellyn reader. The reader said that after being raised in a conservative Christian family, they felt that they could no longer connect with Christianity. Through reading about other forms of spirituality, they were beginning to learn more about Paganism and Wicca. They told me that they felt comfortable with what they were learning, but were afraid to make a change in their faith. The letter went on to explain that this reader lived in a small, isolated, conservative town, which served to complicate their

dilemma. So, with nowhere else to turn, they wrote asking for my advice. I was touched and deeply moved. I was humbled and honored that this person wrote to me, a stranger, asking for help.

Here was someone at a crossroads, someone ready to walk a new path, but they didn't know where, or how, to start. I responded quickly. I explained to them to take small steps, to read as much as they could about Paganism, Wicca, and the Craft. I let them understand that Paganism in its various forms isn't just a faith but also a lifestyle. As far as dealing with family, I told this person to always calmly point out the common ground that both faiths share and, above all, to set an example by living their life in a positive manner.

I ended by letting the reader know I cared and that they could contact me anytime. I never heard from the person again.

That was years ago. But still today, I think of that letter and what may have happened in that situation. Even though the tide is slowly turning, and Paganism and Wicca are slightly more accepted now, it's still a painful struggle for many to find their way back to the Old Religion.

For those of us who have changed our spiritual path, each of us probably has a different story of how the change came about.

This is my story.

It may not be the right way, but it's my way. I firmly believe that change must come from deep within ourselves, but there are times when we all can use a little help finding our way to make that change. This is just one man's story of how I came to walk a new path. In doing so, I found a sense of peace and a more ordered universe. If I help even one other person to walk a new path toward spiritual fulfillment, then I've accomplished my task.

If you're still reading this, then perhaps you're one of the individuals thinking about learning more about Paganism, Wicca, or the Craft. Let me begin by answering a question I frequently hear: "How do I become a Witch/Pagan?" Here is my answer to that question. You don't *become* a Witch or a Pagan; you *are* a Witch/Pagan. Why do I say this? Well, as I mentioned earlier, change comes from inside you. That being the case, somehow, and somewhere, you must have had some questions about your current faith, or you felt something was missing. Or perhaps you were drawn to the occult, mysticism, or the cycles of nature. In some way, the seed was always there—in your spirit. Now that I've said that, I want you to understand that I'm not going to tell you "how" to become a Witch. Instead, I want to help guide you in expanding the feelings you've probably known were always there.

My Path

As a child, I was greatly influenced by my grandparents. My maternal grandmother was Greek Orthodox Christian, and that is the faith I was raised in. I would attend services with my grandmother, but after church when we'd return home, she would, without realizing it, give me my first lessons in Paganism.

She began to tell me stories about the gods and goddesses worshipped by the ancient Greeks. I was mesmerized. I could imagine Ares, the fierce god of war, doing battle, and Zeus sitting on his golden throne atop Mount Olympus, ruling all the gods and goddesses. And, of course, all Greek children know how Athena created the olive tree, and how the council of gods thought it to be such a useful gift to the human race, they decided to name the Greek capital Athens in her honor. Out of these stories I began to see how the religions of the Ancients were more balanced than the Christianity I knew. There were gods—*and* goddesses. There was a balance of male and female energies.

My father's parents were farmers, and as I was growing up, I would spend each summer on their farm. It was there that I began to learn about and understand the natural world. I began to experience first-hand the seasonal energies of the Wheel of the Year. I learned what our Pagan ancestors had known centuries before: that the earth is our Mother and that she sustains us. And being on our family farm helped me develop an awe for the enduring pattern of the seasons. At night I'd walk the fields and gaze at the sky—at the moon and the stars; everything seemed to be in place.

Like most of us who have turned to the Old Religion, I can't pinpoint exactly how or when it happened. Slowly I began a spiritual exploration.

The First Steps

If you're considering changing your faith—not just to Paganism, but to any faith—you must feel that you're moving toward something. If you feel you're running to get away from something or someone, then the time isn't right. And don't do it out of anger.

Don't become a Witch because your dad is so conservative and you think he doesn't understand you, so you feel that by becoming a Witch you'll shock the hell out of him. Don't change your faith just to prove something to someone else. This new path should be about you and only you.

> **If you're considering changing your faith—not just to Paganism, but to any faith—you must feel that you're moving toward something. If you feel you're running to get away from something or someone, then the time isn't right. And don't do it out of anger.**

Also, never, ever feel that Paganism is better than any other way. Don't let anyone think that you feel their religion is wrong. If you do, you'll alienate people you've always loved.

Next, read. Read anything you can about Paganism, Wicca, Witchcraft, and mysticism. There are wonderful

sources online as well as books. Check out authors such as Raymond Buckland, Scott Cunningham, Marion Weinstein, and Doreen Valiente. Read about Native Americans and mystical orders such as the Whirling Dervishes, too. Try to include authors from races and cultures different from your own.

The amount of reading material available today to someone new to the Old Religion is so much greater than what I had. Do you know what was the first book about Witchcraft that I bought? It was a Dell twenty-five-cent paperback titled *Everyday Witchcraft* that I purchased in a grocery store checkout line when I was in college! I'm not kidding. Oh sure, it was just a "pop" witchy sort of book, but I had nowhere else to turn.

If you have a mentor who can guide you when needed, you're fortunate. However, like the reader I mentioned, many of us don't, so books will help fill that void.

Meditation

Solitude and meditation can be helpful during this transitional period in your life. May I suggest that you always ground and center before your meditation sessions? Feel as if roots are connecting your feet to the earth. Quietly speaking appropriate words of power before meditation is also beneficial.

A Word About Magic

If the only reason that you're considering making this change is to perform magic and cast spells, then you're making a mistake. Yes, Witches and some Pagans work positive magic, but magic is only a small part of our faith. As I said, Paganism should be a total lifestyle, which includes respecting nature and all living creatures and honoring the earth and the seasons.

Besides, I know some devout Christians who successfully practice various forms of positive magic. There are also some Christians who have remarkable psychic skills. Remember, it takes more than magical and psychic powers to be a Witch.

Dealing with Family and Friends

First of all, you don't need to tell anyone about your feelings. This is about you. If family and friends begin asking you questions, calmly answer them. Be prepared to tell them that you don't worship Satan! Explain that Satan is a Christian concept. I always point out that many Christian figures such as the Virgin Mary are Christianized versions of Pagan beliefs. So, for example, I've said that the Virgin Mary is the Christian form of the even more ancient Mother Goddess. And I go on to say how interesting it is that one religion builds upon the beliefs of the older faiths. This usually seems to work, and it's true.

Some Final Thoughts

For many of us, our happiest childhood memories center around Christian traditions and decorations—Easter eggs, valentines, and Christmas trees, to name just a few. And some people I've known think they must give up these lovely traditions when they embrace a Pagan way of life. No way! Remember, most of the Christian traditions were originally Pagan—even birthday cakes. So go ahead and dye eggs at Ostara, send a Valentine's Day card, and decorate the Yule tree. When you do, you're remaining true to your Pagan roots.

. . . .

As you begin walking your new path, take comfort in knowing that many have gone before you. They've left their footprints for you to follow, and in turn you'll leave footprints for others to follow. Who knows, the day may come when you'll hold your hand out to someone walking this same path behind you, and you can say, "Here, let me help you. I know the way."

James Kambos *is a solitary. He enjoys researching the folk magic traditions of Appalachia, where he lives. He has a degree in history and geography from Ohio University.*

Illustrator: Kathleen Edwards

Practical Lessons in Kindness and Gratitude from the Grasshopper and the Ant

Barbara Ardinger

This story is presented with apologies to Jean de La Fontaine for significant changes to his fable.

"Curses on that grasshopper!" exclaimed the ever-busy Madame Fourmi. "All he ever does is play. He'll be sorry when winter comes."

And so it went. Every day, Madame Fourmi spent the morning scrubbing her front steps. And Monsieur Cigale?

"Partaaaaayyyyy!" Every day, he sped by on his skateboard. "Hey, Auntie Ant, stop cleaning the concrete and come play with us. We're gonna start a band!"

"Not on your life," muttered this grandmother, most of whose conversations with her many daughters and granddaughters consisted of instructions on how to properly clean their homes and hills and how to prepare and store food for the winter. "Life is serious business, it is, it is. We need to plan ahead."

"Oh, Auntie Ant," Cigale called back. "Lighten up!" Then he called his friends. "Yo, dudes! Let's rock!"

Señor Cockroach and his cousins Vlad and Ludwiggie came first, carrying their Stratocasters. They were followed by young Reb Cicada and Xiansheng Cricket (who had leapt out of his little bamboo cage), both among the world's best percussionists. Next were Gold William and his Fly Boys, ready to do the vocals. Finally, Mighty Dwayne Scorpion arrived.

"At the downbeat," he said as he raised his tail, and then, "Parta-aaaayyyyy!" And the music began. So did other annoying habits of young partying males.

"Life is serious," Madame Fourmi said over and over. "There is no time to play. We must be ready for whatever may come. I'm going to lay a good, heavy hex on those annoying boys. They don't belong here."

First, she tried throwing leaves of dittany of Crete (which drives away venomous beasts) at them, but the boys just ate the leaves and kept playing. She tried angelica to exorcise them. Nothing. Then she threw chunks of pumice and serpentine, which protects against insects. The boys put the stones in their rattles. She sent a gang of fleas to attack them, but the acrobatic bugs just picked up the thumb cymbals and began leaping higher and higher. She stirred up some grasshopperbane and splashed it at them. Nada.

Finally, because the arthropodine band was playing at full volume day and night, she decided to build two new altars upon which to set up banishing spells. She was determined to commit insecticide. The first altar she dedicated to the pale green goddess who rules the night. The second she dedicated to the great orange monarch of the day.

"Great Luna," she prayed at the first new altar, "teach those boys that there is no time for play. Nighttime is for sleeping." And, "O Mother Sun," she also prayed, "teach those boys that we must prepare for winter, or any other disaster that may befall us. Daytime is for working."

Next she stood up and went out to her garden to pick beans and oats and kale to preserve for the winter. She canned tomatoes, carrots, yellow squashes, broccoli, blueberries, eggplants, white asparagus, and blackberries. Then, when she had some spare time again and the band was still playing in the middle of the street, she went back to her two altars.

"Curse those insects!" she cried out. "I hate them, I hate them, I hate them!"

"Daughter," said a quiet voice, "why are you so mean? Who do you think you are? Why do you think you're in charge of other insects?" It was Grandmother Spider. "Daughter," she said, "can we rule anyone except ourselves?"

"I sure can try," said Madame Fourmi. "My intention is good. It's to ensure peace and quiet in the neighborhood. To get rid of those noisy pests who play day and night and never do any serious work. I know what's good for them! They need to be serious like me. They need to learn to plan ahead as I do. They're so noisy—I hate them!"

Grandmother Spider shook her head. Her whole great web shook. "The first thing you must learn," she said, "is to exorcise the word 'hate' from your vocabulary. We must never hate our fellow and sister creatures." She stepped down a strand and came closer to Madame Fourmi. "If someone bothers you, wish them well... *somewhere else*... and focus your mind on another thought. But don't project hate. If you can't project love, project indifference. Indifference is the true opposite of hate." She reached into a bundle in her web. "Burn this sandalwood. Its smoke will clear negativity—and that is certainly what you need to do!"

Because one may not disobey Grandmother Spider, Madame Fourmi burned not only the sandalwood but also some sage and lavender. She walked around her spotless house with the burning herbs. Pretty soon her emotions felt a bit clearer.

But the boys were still playing in the street. Yes, she felt clearer, but she was still seriously annoyed. "I don't hate them," she said, "but I am seriously annoyed by their so-called music. Don't they ever take a break?"

She went back to her second altar. "O Mother Sun, help me make them shut up. Help me make them be quiet and go away."

Carefully avoiding the candles, the Great Orange Butterfly fluttered down to the altar. "Daughter," she said, "do you know the story of the contest between the Sun and Boreas, the North Wind? You don't? Let me tell it to you. There's a lesson in it.

"The two great powers decided to find out who was stronger. There was a fellow standing on the street. The winner would be the one who made the fellow take off his coat. Boreas blew at the fellow on the street. He buttoned up his coat. The North Wind blew and blew, and with every wintry blast, the fellow hugged his coat tighter. Finally Boreas shook his head and stepped back. Now the Sun took pity on the fellow and smiled down at him. After receiving more solar smiles, the fellow took off his coat. 'Well,' said the North Wind, 'I guess a warm smile gets better results than a cold blast.'"

The Butterfly smiled at Madame Fourmi. "That's your lesson for today. Go out and smile at those musicians."

"Are you kidding??"

"I am not kidding. Which would you want coming at you? The wintry blast or the smile of the sun?"

Madame Fourmi got it. She went outside. Although, like Malvolio, she was out of practice where smiling was concerned, she gave it her best try.

Cigale noticed. "Auntie Ant!" he cried. "Good ta see ya! How ya doin'? Keepin' yer cool?"

"Oh, no, it's summertime. Hot weather. I am not keeping cool." But after one of the musicians explained "cool" to her, she nodded. "I guess that's another lesson for me."

"Way to go, Auntie Ant!"

The next day, she said, "Would you boys like some refreshments? You seem to be working—uh, *playing*—very hard." And she brought them some good, healthy herbal tea, which, when she wasn't looking, they diluted with other liquids they had. She also brought

potato chips she'd forgotten she had. The boys promptly got potato chips all over the street and sidewalk.

"I hate—NO, I *am annoyed*—at those bugs." And she brought out her broom. She was very surprised when two of the musicians helped her tidy up the street and sidewalk. Then she remembered something her mother had always told her. "Thank you, boys. Please accept my thanks." Mother was right. Always say please and thank you.

"Way ta go, Auntie Ant! Hey, d'you like music? Whaddaya wanna hear?"

She had to think about that. She and music had never been on friendly terms. Music wasn't serious enough. (She was unfamiliar with the German Romantic composers.) Finally, she said, "Well, I remember hearing some folk songs. How about 'Turn! Turn! Turn!'?"

And the band segued right into it. "To everything, turn, turn, turn, there is a season…"

"Which reminds me," she said when they had finished. "The season will indeed be turning. Are you boys ready for winter? What are you going to do when you get cold and hungry? You can't eat tunes, you know."

It came as no surprise when they admitted they hadn't given the winter a single thought. "We live to play," they said. "Life's short. Enjoy it while you can!"

"Well," said Madame Fourmi, "you boys have some lessons to learn, too. But you know what? I like your folk songs. I don't hate you anymore. Let's see what we can arrange for winter. Since my children all moved out, I have extra rooms in my house. You can rent from me and—"

"—and work for our room and board," said Cigale. "Dudes! Ya think? We can help with the cleaning and wash dishes and reach into places little Auntie Ant can't reach."

And so, to make a long story short, lessons were learned. The musicians learned the importance of planning ahead. More important, Madame Fourmi learned the important lesson of expressing kindness and gratitude. She also got to hear more folk rock, which she learned to like quite a lot.

Barbara Ardinger, PhD (*www.barbaraardinger.com*) *is the author of* Secret Lives, *a novel about crones and other magical folks, and* Pagan Every Day, *a unique daybook of daily meditations. Her other books include* Goddess Meditations (*the first-ever book of meditations focusing on goddesses*), Finding New Goddesses (*a parody of goddess encyclopedias*), *and an earlier novel,* Quicksilver Moon (*which is realistic…except for the vampire*). *Her monthly blogs appear on her website and on* Feminism and Religion (*http://feminismandreligion.com*), *where she is a regular Pagan contributor. Her work has also been published in devotionals to Isis, Athena, and Brigid. Barbara lives in Long Beach, California, with her two rescued Maine coon cats, Schroedinger and Heisenberg.*

Illustrator: Tim Foley

Leaving a Legacy in the Pagan Community

Boudica Foster

When someone dies, it's customary to review the deceased's life and highlight their accomplishments and successes. The Pagan community is no exception. When we lose one of our elders or community members, we discuss what they did to make the community better. The highlights of the individual's life are usually pondered and added to the general knowledge of the community. I remember when Doreen Valiente died, discussions of her involvement in the British community were common, and her life was one of those that we hold up to the community as worth knowing and remembering. The same was true when Isaac Bonewits and Margot Adler passed; people remember their many contributions to the community and organizations. Judy Harrow left her library as a gift to the Pagan community.

We also have those we would rather forget. Every community has had at least one member who crossed the line. The Pagan community

has had members we would like to purge from memory simply because they proved to be a pox on the community and their contributions were more scandals than anything else. We have had a few "leaders" we regretted as well.

What about our contributions to the community? Each of us contributes in some way to our local community. Whether it's that potluck dish that everyone begs you to bring to circles and sabbats or the personalized and professional spiritual counseling you provide to your group, you will be remembered for something in your local community.

What do you want to be remembered for? You do have a choice, you know. How much involvement do you have in your local community? You don't have to be an elder or a facilitator to leave behind a legacy to your local community. You need not be a high priestess of a coven or the founder of a tradition to be remembered as a great person by your friends and community members.

It's the simple things that people really remember when it comes to community. We remember the help we received, or the kindness of a person when we were in need, or just a person who made us smile. It's the unassuming things that we remember, not the grand things that we read about all the time.

Some of you might be thinking, why be remembered at all? That's a good question—do you consider it worth being remembered for anything? Well, that's part of what a community does—we remember those who have gone before us. We remember our community members and keep their presence alive within our groups. After all, isn't that what Samhain is all about? We don't just remember our family or close friends; we also remember those in our community and those with whom we spent time. Hopefully we remember them with fondness. It's like a family; we remember our ancestors and we either smile at the thought or we wish we had never gone there. Yes, if you are involved in a community of any kind, there will be those who will remember you. Some of our community family members we will remember with fondness, while others we will remember with a grimace.

It is pretty much the same with the Pagan community online. We remember those we interact with, and we discuss them because we belong to the online community. This is true for many solitary Pagans who only interact with the community online. Their impressions of us come from interaction online with one another. And yes, there is a legacy when we discuss Pagans online. It can be pretty much the same as in real life, especially when you are discussing the better known

Pagans. I remember Ellen Cannon Reed; she was a great teacher of her own tradition and was a fantastic writer whom I respect. And yes, we did talk online and she was an amazing woman. She was of the old-school traditions, and I consider myself very progressive. This caused some ruffled feathers occasionally, but that does not mean I did not like her. Rather, I found her work to be a good foundation for those who were new to the Pagan paths, and I sent a number of students to her online workshops and classes. She left me with some of her experiences that I recall even today, and I still use the lessons she left me.

Remembering big-name Pagans is easy. Whether through art, books, community events, festivals, or defending religious rights, they are very visible and we see them on websites, on social media, and in the news doing things that benefit our community.

But the really special people are the regular folks we encounter. I have facilitated many community events over the years. I remember potluck dinners at community welcoming events that were feasts extraordinaire. I always looked forward to doing a community event for some groups because they could cook! I also remember some groups that I have been part of over the years—wonderful gatherings with extraordinary people and discussions that made me think and led me to ponder the mysteries of the universe. And I remember that without the help and support of the members, the events would not have been as successful or memorable.

I also remember people I would rather forget. We don't always meet people we like. There have been some who clearly were not right in the head. It may or may not have been their fault. It's not for me to judge; it's between them and their gods. But they have left me regretting some choices to be very accepting. I tend to err on the side of wait and see rather than writing someone off at the first encounter. And while it's an honorable thing to allow individuals to

prove themselves, sometimes the proof can be staggering. We cannot avoid this. We encounter this in any community of which we are members. It's something we have to learn to accept. We don't like it, but these people are everywhere. It's up to us to make sure they do not disrupt our communities and to decide, as a community, what is to be done about them.

How are you going to be remembered by your community? What legacy will you leave behind? What is it that makes you unique, and what is it that you want to achieve in your community?

I know a few people who have extended themselves above and beyond whenever the need was there. They were not high priests or high priestesses. They weren't elders or even what most people would consider key people in the community. I consider these folks to be essential to the workings of any community. They are the quiet organizers, the movers and deliverers of finished work. They are the backbone of any good community. They are always there. They always lend a hand. They are willing to go the extra mile for their friends and for all members of their community.

These members drive people around, pick people up, and take time to make sure we have all the supplies we need for our community events. They make arrangements and reservations, they clean up after events, they do dishes…the list is endless. These people are the tireless workers who are essential to making our communities run smoothly. They are the letter writers, the phone call makers; they remember appointments, names, and all the little details without having to be reminded. Without them, our communities would fall apart. They are the cohesion in our communities. And they leave a legacy that is just as great, if not greater, than some of those big-name Pagans we have.

What is sad is that sometimes we wait until someone is dead to recognize their efforts on our behalf. In some cases, we don't recognize them at all. I am a firm believer in telling people what a great help they have been and making sure they are recognized for their efforts. Maybe we need to do this more within our communities. I certainly feel this is a necessary step toward making our communities feel more welcoming and inviting. There is nothing like publicly acknowledging someone's assistance in front of the whole group or in front of the entire organization. Always give credit where credit is due.

We also should respect those who are constantly in the front doing more than anyone else. We tend to think of community elders as individuals who have traveled the entire path and achieved status and respect, but I also believe that some people have a place supporting those individuals who go the full path. High priests and high priestesses achieve this status with the support of the individuals who make up their community. Recognition for any service to a community should include being elevated to elder status for playing a supporting role in building and maintaining community, and these members should have the ability to teach and pass on their skills to promising individuals. People in service need to have mentors, encouragement, and titles just as much as those who run the show. While a high priestess may have greater responsibilities, the people who provide kitchen duty or order the supplies serve in much-needed positions as well and shoulder responsibilities that are key to the growth of the community. I know that some groups recognize all their members, and we would do well to take a page from their book and express respect and admiration for those who serve in quiet ways.

Then we have those who have left a dark mark on our communities. There are those who would like to sweep these individuals under the rug and never mention them again. Sometimes what these people have done can be so hard on a community that it causes suffering, distress, emotional unrest, and even the breakup of a group. But we, as individuals, should never forget their names or what they have done. These people can and do disrupt other groups, and we, as responsible individuals, should make sure they do not repeat what they have done.

In some cases, what they may have done is illegal, and I have seen groups ignore these people rather than report them to the proper authorities. I must say that this is not the way to go. Experience shows that an individual who breaks the law in one group will do so in

another if given the chance. We need to take responsibility and turn these individuals over to law enforcement and press charges. It's not an easy thing to do, and sometimes it can be just as emotionally upsetting as the offense itself. But knowing that these individuals will never do this again to anyone else should be reassuring enough to make our efforts worthwhile. It also shows the rest of society that we are the same as they are—and that we will stand by the laws of the social system just as they do.

There are also the "gray line" members. These people are members of the community who may have presented us with a good or important message, but whose life choices are less than respectable. I know a well-known event organizer who has a less-than-sterling reputation for being honest. Actually, I can say I have known a few group leaders whom I would classify as not being all that honest. Some are still working in the community; some have been released from positions of responsibility and are no longer involved in any community.

I have known some leaders in a few organizations over the years who exhibited personal behavior that would be considered socially unacceptable or illegal. How do we handle these kinds of people? Do we allow these people to be remembered as respected members of the community because they exhibited organizational or leadership skills yet are personally questionable?

My question is this: If these people were outside the Pagan community and were members of your social community or political representatives of your community, would you allow them to represent your community or be considered part of your community if it was also known that they were dishonest or had questionable leadership skills or personal backgrounds?

This is a discussion each community needs to have and resolve to the satisfaction of that community. We need to take a clear stand in regard to how we, as a community, want to be remembered, because a community leaves a legacy to its membership and to society. A tainted board of directors, a few trustees who were not trustworthy, individuals who pushed personal agendas rather than goals that benefited the group—we need to push these types of people away from us and cap these kinds of behavior. Many times these are the underlying reasons why groups and organizations fail—the group as a whole did not act to curb an individual's personal behavior and it brought down the entire group. We have to be tough and not allow behavior in our Pagan communities that we would not allow in our social circles or other outside communities.

I think, in the long run, that if we show we are the same as any other community—that we encounter issues just like all other communities and we deal with them on the same level as other communities do—it will go a long way in showing that we are as law-abiding as everyone else. We need to show that the similarities between us are greater than the differences. We should set an example as a community that we recognize the contributions of all individual members on a regular basis and we do not wait for them to die to recognize the parts they play in our communities. Yes, we are also rebels, and we will continue to work for change in our society, but we are also law-abiding citizens and we have the same good things, and bad things, as everyone else does. After all, isn't this how we are with each other under the Pagan umbrella? Leaving this kind of legacy for our future members is worth more than any individual contribution because it shows that we can work together as a community, within the confines of the same laws that the rest of society follows.

What will be your legacy to your community? What would you like to be remembered for? We should make sure that those who are essential to our communities are respected and acknowledged for their work. You don't have to be a big-name Pagan to leave a positive legacy in your community. Sometimes all it takes is being there when needed.

Boudica Foster *is best known for her professional reviews of books on Paganism and its various paths. Boudica and her husband, Michael, ran the successful* Wiccan/Pagan Times *website and Facebook page. She also ran the* Zodiac Bistro *website, a repository of articles, commentaries, and reviews, for many years till she retired that recently as well. She is a self-published author.*

Boudica is a staunch supporter of building Pagan community and has worked in covens as well as having a solitary practice. She has presented at many events in the Northeast and Ohio. She still presents occasionally at events and holds public workshops in the Northeast. She runs the blog-style website boudica.net, an online bookstore, and reads tarot cards for clients. Boudica lives in Bucks County, PA, with her husband of many years and her cats. Visit her online at www.boudica.net/wp.

Illustrator: Bri Hermanson

A Place in the Sun: The *Lur* of the Nordic Bronze Age

Linda Raedisch

Welcome to the Nordic Bronze Age! We hope you enjoy your stay. The NBA is both a time and a place, encompassing southern Scandinavia as well as Germany's Baltic Coast in the years 1730 to 760 BCE, give or take. It's warmer and drier here than in the twenty-first century. Most of the land has been worked into farms and gardens interrupted only by the odd coppice, rock escarpment, or grave mound, so you'll enjoy wide vistas over the fields and out to sea. This is the setting in which you'll witness ancient Paganism in action.

You'll rely on your host family to look after you, so it's best to start out on the right foot. Your Temporal Travel Agent's costume rental service has just what you need. For the mature woman, we suggest a short-sleeved woolen blouse and full-length gathered skirt. Teenage girls can get away with a string miniskirt, but don't forget the spiked bronze belt disc: this will serve to discourage rambunctious NBA boys. Compared to the cowed ladies of ancient Greece, the NBA woman enjoys a fair amount of freedom and respect. No veils here—just a lightweight netted bonnet. You can have fun picking out such items as spiral bracelets, earrings, wire torques, and amber beads when you visit the local craftsmen.

Gentlemen, please note that pants have not yet been invented; you'll have to make do with a linen loin cloth covered by a long tunic or cloak. Unfortunately, visitors to the NBA are not permitted to wear swords or the bronze horned helmets of warriors. As a member of

the traveling merchant caste, you will wear a felt cap. Both men and women will be issued a short bronze dagger for spearing meat, peeling fruit, or whittling sticks, as well as for self-defense. Moccasin-type footwear is acceptable throughout the NBA.

Hopefully, you are already studying your phrase book. Remember, Danish, Swedish, Norwegian, and German are not yet spoken. If you want to be understood, you will have to use Proto-Germanic. Within Proto-Germanic there are several dialects, so if you plan to spend part of your stay in, say, Egtved, Denmark, before going to view the rock carvings at Tanum in Sweden, you will need more than one phrase book. And while you'll find plenty of rowboats, cattle, and human figures carved into the rocks, you won't see any runes: this is a pre-literate society.

Accommodations

"Home," for the elite, is a thatched longhouse with an open hearth and very little furniture. At times, the smoke will be so thick you'll have trouble finding your bed, which is little more than a pile of blankets on the floor. Close to the house, you may notice a hawthorn or crabapple

tree. Do not allow your children to climb it unless you observe your host's children doing so. This is the original "family tree," and there could be an ancestor buried among its roots.

Those little striped piglets you see running around the kitchen garden are destined eventually for the cook pot. While meat is for special occasions, porridge is served at all meals. If you are visiting the Late Bronze Age, your hostess may proudly serve you oatmeal—it's the latest thing! Cows have been around since the time of the Beaker people, so you can always get fresh milk, cheese, and something not dissimilar to yogurt.

Berries can be eaten fresh, but apples, which are small, hard, and sour, should be stewed or drunk in the form of hard cider. There is also mead and beer flavored with a variety of herbs, though not hops. Be sure to sample the Danish NBA specialty of wheat beer sweetened with honey and blueberries.

On the Trail of the Elves

One of the most common questions visitors to the NBA ask is, "Will we see elves?" The best place to glimpse an elf is at one of the many cup-marked stones, or "elf stones," as they are known in Scandinavia today. There is no shortage of them. If you have chosen the Sam Gamgee Tour, you'll be traveling from stone to stone, arriving at a new one each evening—the best time to see elves. Keep your eye on the constellations: some believe the cup-marks are actually star charts.

Some of these stones will already be ancient at the time of your visit, such as the famous *Schalenstein von Bunsoh* in northern Germany, whose "cups" were pecked out during the New Stone Age, about 2500 BCE. In addition to the cup-marks, which are made to hold offerings, there is a four-spoked wheel representing the sun, a set of handprints, and a footprint. The footprint indicates the presence of an unseen deity, or, if you like, an elf.

Elves are associated with both the brilliance of the sun and the darkness of the underworld through which the sun must pass each night. There will be a lot of bustling activity around these stones as would-be mothers come to petition the resident spirits, pouring out milk and honey and placing flickering rush-lights in the hollows.

Stones marked with footprints, which may be filled in with red ochre, are also the focus of fertility rites. When making offerings at these sites, take your cue from the locals. The substance offered may determine whether the unseen powers grant you a boy or a girl.

Occasionally, infants are abandoned in the vicinity of these stones. Do not attempt an inter-temporal adoption! In the NBA imagination, these children are born from the stone itself and are therefore the gifts of the elves. They will be given a privileged upbringing in the village.

Festivals and Funerals

You should plan your visit so you'll be able to take in at least one communal feast. Your travel agent can pinpoint for you when the observances later known as Walpurgis Night (April 30) and Whitsunday (in late spring) are going to occur. Solstices and equinoxes are also big party nights. Three thousand years ago, bonfires were built and sacred dances performed in honor of the sun on the flat, stage-like tops of the barrows. Swept up in the action of an NBA festival, you might, for an instant, imagine you are in India, but instead of the bright orange Asian marigold, you will see blue flax flowers, yellow broom, crabapple blossoms, yarrow, honeysuckle, or mistletoe draped over the celebrants, the cattle, and, in the case of a funeral, the coffin.

The colors might be muted, but the spirits of the celebrants are in no way dampened as they dance to the sound of flutes, drums, and the deep bovine lowing of *lurs*, sinuous bronze trumpets that are played on all formal occasions and always in pairs. In the background blazes the all-important element of fire, the earthly embodiment of the sun. If you attend one of the solstice events, you may see, trundling around the village, a life-size version of the famous bronze Trundholm Chariot, which depicts a horse pulling an elaborately incised golden sun disc mounted on a chariot.

If you want to witness the raising of an NBA grave mound, you should visit the Early to Middle Bronze Age when interment with grave goods is the rule, at least among the elite. Later, people begin to cremate the dead, burying the ashes in pottery urns. No one form of burial was ever universal in the NBA, but after 1300 BCE, cremation is more or less the norm. Don't be surprised if you see some very sooty people hanging around the urnfields. They are not ghosts, but members of a hereditary class charged with stoking the ever-burning funeral fires, as India's low-caste "Lords of Death" do today.

If you want to be sure to witness the hullabaloo of an NBA funeral, book your visit for the summer of 1370 BCE in what is now the town of Egtved, Denmark. Tree-ring dating of Egtved Girl's oak coffin tells us it was in this year that she was laid to rest. Tell your travel agent you want to arrive just as the yarrow is coming into bloom, for yarrow flowers were also enclosed in the coffin. We don't know what the circumstances were surrounding the death of twenty-year-old Egtved Girl, or that of the six-year-old child whose ashes were buried with her. Were they mother and child, dying of the same illness, or was the child dispatched in order to wait on the older girl in the afterlife? Keep in mind that prehistory is what it is, and the denizens of the NBA would no doubt be horrified at certain goings-on of our own.

Vanaheim on Earth

On a summer day three thousand years ago, the wind sighs and ripples through the barley. Rise up on your toes, and you can glimpse the sparkling wavelets of a becalmed sea. Such a day is as close as you'll get to the sacred realm of Vanaheim, home to the Vanir, the salty old fertility god Frey, his sister Freya, and their father Njord. On this day, the Viking god Odin has not yet arrived from the east, and if it's Thor's hammer you're looking for, you're about a thousand years too early.

Thor may already be present, but he's no more than a gnome lurking in an oak tree.

It is some time around that pivotal year of 1300 BCE that our Nordic friends begin to look skyward, their eyes following the smoke from the funeral pyre. At this point, the sky god Tyr rises to prominence, though perhaps not yet by that name. Throughout the landscape, you will come across many groves, springs, and low hills devoted to him. Birds are revered, especially waterfowl, along with the sacred ship motif that never seems to go out of style. The sun continues to loom large, depicted as a disc born across the sky in a chariot or a boat with a graceful swan's head at each end.

While the ashes of the dead are enclosed in the earth, their spirits are allowed to escape to the clouds. They don't go empty-handed; bronze swords, daggers, and lurs, along with golden vessels, are cast into the rivers, lakes, and swamps that serve as portals to the otherworld—no longer a place to carry on as one did in life, but an entirely new realm of existence.

Gods and goddesses come and go, new rituals are invented and old ones discarded (when was the last time you heard a lur played at a funeral?), but those ageless, radiant elves are a constant in the Nordic landscape, flourishing all the way from the New Stone Age into our own twenty-first century. No matter which part of the NBA you visit, you'll find ordinary folk honoring and exchanging gifts with these indispensable spirits.

Okay, But Really

The history of the Germanic peoples does not begin until late in the Iron Age when they came into conflict with Rome. I've never had any trouble relating to my Iron Age ancestors, because (a) the Romans wrote about them and (b) the 2,000-year-old sacrificial victim known as Tollund Man, whose body was preserved in a Danish peat bog, is the spitting image of my grandmother. But it was not until I started paging through my uncle's book collection during a visit to northern Germany that I discovered that magical word: *Bronzezeit*. In English, the words "Bronze  Age" conjure up images of Homeric Greece, but *Bronzezeit*, to me, means golden sun discs, amber beads, finely netted caps, and, most of all, barrows.

My uncle happened to have a map of all the Neolithic and Bronze Age grave mounds in the neighborhood. So off we went down the country lanes, fields of barley and rapeseed on the one hand and the quietly sighing Baltic on the other. This was back in the 1990s, and the mounds have since become jumbled in my mind. One was topped by boulders, another covered in grass and difficult to make out over the shoulders of the cows grazing around it, as they must already have done back in the NBA. Yet another barrow stood in the middle of a field of broccoli. I scraped a bit of moss from the rocks, frightening a russet fawn from the underbrush as I clambered over this unexcavated house of the dead.

You don't have to build a time machine or even buy a plane ticket to experience the Nordic Bronze Age. If you're interested, there are plenty of books on the subject, but you can also do something as simple as lighting a candle and pouring milk over a stone. Make your offering in the evening, when the shadows are long, and you are sure to see elves.

Bibliography/Suggested Reading

Cunliffe, Barry. *Europe between the Oceans: 9000 BC–AD 1000.* New Haven, CT: Yale University Press, 2008. (You can't go wrong with Sir Barry, even if his books do weigh more than a small car.)

Glob, P. V. *Denmark: An Archaeological History from the Stone Age to the Vikings.* Translated from the Danish by Joan Bulman. Ithaca, NY: Cornell University Press, 1971. (Glob was most famous for his study of Iron Age bog mummies, but he also had a foot in the Bronze Age.)

Landeck, Horst-Dieter. *Steine, Gräber, Kultplätze: Ein Reisebegleiter zu mystischen Orten im nördlichen Schleswig-Holstein.* Heide, Germany: Boyens, 2004. (That's German for *Stones, Graves, Cult Sites: A Travel Companion to Mystical Places of Northern Schleswig-Holstein.* While the Bronze Age sites of Denmark are well treated in English, the ones just over the border in Germany are not.)

Manco, Jean. *Ancestral Journeys: The Peopling of Europe from the First Venturers to the Vikings.* New York: Thames and Hudson, 2013. (A smoothly readable blend of the genetic, linguistic, and archaeological evidence.)

Oliver, Neil. *The Vikings: A New History.* New York: Pegasus Books, 2013. (The author takes a good look at the Vikings' Bronze Age ancestors in chapter two, "Stone, Bronze, and Iron.")

Linda Raedisch's *most recent book for Llewellyn is* The Old Magic of Christmas: Yuletide Traditions for the Darkest Days of the Year. *She is also a frequent contributor to Llewellyn's annuals, focusing on prehistory, religion, and lifeways, especially in the northern realms. She moonlights as an instructor in traditional paper crafts, runes, hieroglyphs, and other secret scripts. Her third book will appear in August 2017, by which time she will once more have traveled to the Nordic Bronze Age and back again.*

Illustrator: Christa Marquez

Pagan Standard Time (PST):
A Tale for Tolerance

Monica Crosson

It was on a brilliantly blue morning in July when the clouds had finally parted in the Pacific Northwest that I received a phone call. My friend Marilyn's voice rang with a sweetness that was unlike her typical impish greeting. "Hello, my lovely," she said.

"Hey, Marilyn, what's up?"

"Would you be interested in two tickets to S. J. Tucker this Saturday evening?"

"Uh, yeah." S. J. Tucker was one of my favorite artists, a guitarist and singer who weaves stories with her songs that are fun, thought-provoking, and beautiful.

"How much?" I asked.

"Forty bucks."

"I'll take them. Where's she performing?"

"She and Betsy Tinny will be playing together at a fairie ball in Index.

"Wow, Index. That's a jaunt."

"It'll be fun. Costumes are optional, so you can dress up if you like."

"Awesome," I replied.

I spent the rest of the day absorbing every ray of that stranger called the sun. I pulled weeds until I thought I would pass out, picked raspberries, and harvested peas. As I worked, I thought about the fairie ball and how cool it would be to finally see Sooj (as S. J. is known by friends and dorky superfans like me) in person.

But who would I take with me? My closest friend was spending the summer in Alaska, and my husband was going on a rafting trip with his brother. My coven mates were busy with weddings, vacations, and family reunions.

When the phone rang later that afternoon, I was stretched out on a lawn chair with a book.

"What are you up to?" It was my sister, Angela, who is less than two years my junior. We homeschooled our kids together, shared a lot of the same interests, and even worked together on Saturdays, along with Marilyn, as substitute drivers for our local post office.

"Sitting on my butt, right now," I said.

"What are you doing this Saturday evening? I was thinking of having a barbecue."

"Actually, I'm going with Marilyn and Alex to a fairie ball in Index. S. J. Tucker is playing."

"Is that that kind-of hippie music Marilyn plays at work?"

I laughed. "I don't know if I'd call it 'hippie' music, but yeah."

"I like her stuff. Why didn't she ask me?" Angela's irritation was evident.

"Probably because she thought it would be a little too *Pagan* for you."

You see, the only difference between my sister and me is that she is a fundamentalist Christian—the religion of our youth. It was hard for me, a true child of nature, to grasp onto this faith. As a child, I questioned the malevolency of the Christian God who would deny my beloved pets entrance into heaven and didn't have room for the fairies I insisted lived in our garden.

As a teen, I tried desperately to believe. I attended youth conferences preaching against premarital sex and rock music. I was even president of our youth group for a short time. But always deep within the cobweb-coated creases of my mind, the fairie songs of my childhood still played.

As I reached adulthood, a longing for the ancient ways tickled, until one rain-soaked night in February over twenty years ago, I dedicated myself to the Goddess, and I have never looked back. The problem

One rain-soaked night in February over twenty years ago, I dedicated myself to the Goddess, and I have never looked back. The problem was, I never told my extended family about my spiritual awakening.

was, I never told my extended family about my spiritual awakening, choosing to raise my family in the old ways tucked behind broom closet doors.

As my sister continued her rant about why she never got invited to anything, I mulled over the harm a fairie ball would have on her Christian soul…none. Yes, Sooj was a Pagan artist, but not all of her music was about the Craft. And for crying out loud, it wasn't being held at an esbat. "You know, you should go."

"I don't want your pity invite," she said with a laugh. "You guys have fun."

"Ang, I really would love for you to go. I just wasn't sure whether you'd want to go."

"I would love to go!"

"Great," I said. "Let's meet at Marilyn's after work Saturday. Wear something spritely."

The night of the fairie ball rolled in light and lovely. Angela and I both dressed up. I was an earthy tangle of black, gray, green, and tangerine, while Ang was sunny and bright in pale yellow splashed with turquoise and a chaplet of daisies.

Marilyn and Alex found Marilyn's parents, whom they had planned on meeting in the parking area, which left Angela and me to walk the winding tree-lined drive together. After a few twists and turns, I began to hear the far-off tinkling sound of the penny whistle and the soft chattering of people having a good time. I smiled.

As we rounded the last bend, I was surprised by what we saw. Instead of a gathering of fairie-festooned folk enjoying themselves in an open area near the banks of the woolly Skykomish River, the costumed revelers were gathered around the front entrance of a church of sorts. *What a pretty church*, I thought, looking at the stained-glass pentacle toward the peak… Stained-glass pentacle?! For the love of the Goddess, what had I done? That's when I read the plaque:

Aquarian Tabernacle Church (ATC). Wow, not only had I brought my sister to a Pagan gathering, but it was at one of the largest Wiccan churches in the United States. Awesome.

As we waited in the ticket line, I nervously took note of the ritual jewelry decorating almost everyone and the Pagan symbolism that dotted the grounds—a Green Man hanging on the garden gate that would lead us to the festivities, small altars lit with candles, statuary Goddess figures tucked beneath ferns, and, beyond the gate, a Pagan reading room and prayer flags that swayed on a honey-scented breeze. I should have lovingly pulled my sister aside and clued her in on our location, but I didn't. I justified my decision by telling myself that she knew Sooj was a Pagan artist and she still had wanted to come along. She would be fine. She had probably figured it out, anyway. Yeah, I told myself, it was all good.

. . . .

As we entered ATC's grounds, I marveled over their layout and took mental notes on garden designs. I admired their circle, paved with brick, with a wonderful fire pit in the middle. I became absolutely giddy as I spied Sooj hanging out near the small rustic stage tucked just beyond the circle. But my giddiness soon turned to uneasiness when I caught the nervous glint in my sister's eyes.

"There's Marilyn and Alex," I said, trying to cut the tension. "Let's sit by them."

We spread ourselves out on the cool green grass, and as the fingers of a summer breeze played with my hair, I people-watched. A harem of girls in belly-dance attire chatted under a tree festooned with twinkle lights, steampunk-inspired revelers shared drinks at the bar, and a bevy of forest fairies, of every age and body type, flitted and danced about.

A pot-bellied Pan chugged from a drinking horn, then laughed heartily, making my sister noticeably uncomfortable. She looked at me impatiently from under the shadow of his great white belly, then asked, "When is this thing starting?"

"I don't know," I said. "It was supposed to start at seven."

"Yeah." She glanced at her watch. "It's seven thirty."

"We're on PST here," a masculine voice offered. We both glanced up to find the pot-bellied Pan was talking to us.

"PST," he repeated.

Angela shot me a confused sideways look.

I shrugged. But inside, I was dying because I knew exactly what it meant. I had heard the term PST (Pagan Standard Time) used at plenty of events that were running late, and frankly, I hated the excuse.

"Pacific Standard Time," she mumbled. "Of course we're on Pacific Standard Time." Her brows were knitted and I knew she wasn't going to let this go. I watched as she glanced about, absorbing her surroundings. Then she turned once again to the pot-bellied Pan and asked, "What did you mean by 'PST'?"

He lifted his drinking horn, and amber liquid sloshed from its rim. "Pagan Standard Time!"

I dropped my head and sighed. "Sorry," I said. "I really didn't know until we got here and…"

"I can't be here!" Angela had cut me off. "I'm sorry, but I can't be here," she repeated. The words were shaky and desperate. Before I had time to react, she was off the

grass and spinning around aimlessly, all the while mumbling, "Jesus, forgive me."

"Angie, it's okay," I said, and got up to follow.

As she moved, her wings bounced about erratically. I could feel mine doing the same. Finally, the movement stopped when my wings got wound up in my long hair. I was embarrassed and angered by my sister's reaction. Okay, so she's at a Pagan event. How many times had my kids been invited to *parties* only to find out later they were Christian events? And what about the prayers that were thrust upon me during low times in my life, even when I politely declined them?

I caught up with Angela as she was about to hit a vendor's table. Pentacles gleamed from ritual jewelry and from the covers of journals that were set out for sale.

"Demons are surrounding me!" she yelled, spotting the items.

I quickly grabbed her by the wings and led her toward the gate.

Once on the gravel drive, she said, "Monica, those are Witches. I'm sorry, but I can't support that." She crossed her arms.

"I paid for the tickets." I said, trying desperately to keep hold of my temper. "You're not *supporting* anything."

"No, I can't be in there," she continued. "God does not want me in there. I want to go home."

"Well, you know Marilyn and Alex aren't leaving, so I think we're stuck here." I could hear the crowd cheer and then S. J. Tucker and Betsy Tinny were introduced. Music began to fill the air, and with the realization that I wasn't going to see Sooj, my heart sunk.

We walked together toward the main road. The sound of Betsy Tinny's haunting cello music rode the breeze—a bittersweet sound to my ears.

Angela pointed to bumper stickers we hadn't spotted on the walk in and exclaimed, "More pentagrams—Satan's symbol!" She shook her head.

"No," I said softly, "there's no devil in the Craft."

She recognized the line from the movie *Practical Magic* and cracked a weak smile.

"You know, Ang, those are just people," I said, pointing back toward the party. "They're worshipping their deities, just like you do. Nobody is sacrificing children."

"The Bible is very clear on Witchcraft, Monica."

"Yeah!" I had finally lost control. "It's clear on a lot of things. Mostly a lot of barbaric and cruel nonsense. What kills me is that most of its contents are ignored unless it suits your purpose." I was shaking. "Have you people actually read your own holy book?"

She looked at me for a long time. It was apparent to me that I had hurt her, and I felt horrible. "Yes," she finally said, "I have."

We walked in silence until the sound of Sooj's music was just a faint reminder of what could have been. When we reached the main road, we plopped down on a fallen log.

"Go ahead and go back," she said. "I'll be fine."

"No, I'm not leaving you here alone."

"Monica," she said as a tear rolled down her cheek, "go and enjoy your show."

I patted her shoulder. "I said I wasn't leaving."

"You know, we've always known you and your family were into this stuff," she said, pointing back toward the ATC. "I don't know why you didn't just tell us."

I chuckled. "Probably because I knew how everyone would react."

"You haven't been that kind, either. Do you think we don't notice the eye rolls and snide remarks at the holidays?"

I shook my head. "You're right. I need to be more sensitive. But you guys have to quit giving my kids Christian-oriented gifts and inviting them to religious events."

She smiled and grabbed my hand. "Deal."

"Come on," I said. "Let's go for a walk."

"Where to?"

I shrugged. "Town is about three miles that way," I said, pointing. "Let's go check it out."

So as bats began to flit across the inky sky, two forty-something-year-old women in fairy costumes paraded into the tiny, picturesque town of Index.

"So," my sister said, with her arm wrapped through mine as we walked, "help me learn a little about what you believe."

"Really?" I asked.

She smiled. "Yeah."

We sat at a picnic table in front of an old-fashioned country store and drank diet sodas as I taught my sister the basic workings and symbolism of Wicca.

By the time we returned, the moon was peeking over cragged trees and a slight chill stung the air. We went to Marilyn and Alex's jeep, in hopes that they had unlocked it. They had. Angela got in. "Go," she said. "Catch whatever's left of the concert. I promise, I'm fine."

I shook my head and ran back to the ATC. As I made my way in, Sooj was preparing to play her final song. How appropriate, I thought, that it was "Witches' Rune."

The fire pit had been lit, and it jumped and sparked. Soon revelers were dancing around it as Sooj's ethereal voice filled the air. I joined the dancers, and as I spun and swayed, tears filled my eyes. I am a Witch—out of the shadows and proud.

Practice What You Preach

Practicing religious tolerance can be challenging, even for the most forward-minded of us, and sadly, religious dissension has been part of America's DNA since the Mayflower landed on Plymouth Rock. One of the main reasons for the discord is that our faith traditions (or lack thereof) often define a significant part of our personal identity, and it's easy to become defensive. Understanding religious beliefs other than our own is a key element of tolerance and is essential to understanding both our nation and the world.

It is easy to overreact in an inappropriate manner when discussing matters of faith, because an essential part of religious freedom is the right to reject what is not true for you. Here are some tips for practicing religious tolerance:

- Remain calm and respectful. You are setting a healthy example.

- Set boundaries with people who insist on lecturing you or who claim that their way is the only way. Walk away if the person becomes insulting or abusive.

- Take time to learn about religions other than your own.

- Remember, you do not need to agree with another person's doctrine of choice; you only need to recognize the importance of it in the person's life.

- Take your family to a religious service of another faith, or ask someone of another faith to speak about their beliefs.

. . . .

My sister and I now laugh about "PST," and we both feel that the experience has made us closer. This year, she gave me some ideas for one of my family's sabbat celebrations, and I helped make props for her Sunday school play. And though she still would probably never attend another Pagan event, we are planning to go see Sooj the next time she performs at a cafe or bookstore. I can respect that.

Sources

Sonya Bruyette, www.dailyom.com/library/000/000/000000683.html, 2006.

Religious Tolerance, www.religioustolerance.org.

Monica Crosson *is a Master Gardener who lives in the beautiful Pacific Northwest, happily digging in the dirt and tending her raspberries with her husband, three kids, two goats, two dogs, three cats, a dozen chickens, and Rosetta the donkey. She has been a practicing Witch for twenty years and is a member of Blue Moon Coven. Monica writes fiction for young adults and is the author of* Summer Sage.

Illustrator: Rik Olson

Discordianism: A Taste of April Foolery All Year Round

Jymi x/ø ("Reverend Variable")

The bride and groom wanted us to officiate a Discordian ceremony for them…and that was the last thing anyone was absolutely sure about.

The venue changed two or three times. The day was set for a Saturday. No, a Friday. No, the next week Friday. No, the original Saturday. I swear. I sweartagawd it was supposed to be Saturday. Luckily I heard my phone ringing in the midst of band rehearsal twenty miles away on Friday night when the bride called: they were in town, they were in their costumes, and when should they expect us to come and collect them from their hotel room because the ceremony was going to start in two hours?

But then things came together and we lived happily ever after, dancing the night away beneath the sigil of the Elder Gods.

When you're planning for Discord, you get what you ask for. Leave plenty of room for improv.

1. What Is Discordianism?

Well, it's not "eeeeevil," or even what I personally would call "dark." Discord is an off-note, a hiccup, a glitch in the system, a big smeary Wad of Chaos scraped off the bottom of the Sneeze Guard on the Salad Bar of Order.

At best, one could say that it's the opposite of harmony, order, and (what some may call) perfection. However, there's a large gray area between perfect harmony and total discord, so at any point in between, we must depend on our individual perceptions to tell us how much of each quality is present.

Are Discordians involved in "black magic"? Sure, some of them are, but they've probably distorted the original instructions to the point where you can't tell what color they are anymore.

Are Discordians dangerous? That depends on the Discordian, and on what you would call "danger."

Some Discordians seek to disrupt (or destroy) expectations so that what IS can be re-formed. But is there anything that IS, outside of individual observation and expectation, or does reality arrive à la

Descartes: "I think it is, therefore it is." Ask other Discordians what they think, too. You'll get a wide range of answers, and possibly a poke in the eye, or ice cream.

2. Is Discordianism a Joke?

Absolutely not.

3. The Scientific Perspective

From Earth's weather patterns, to the thermodynamic behavior of humongous balls of space gas, to Jupiter's Great Red Spot, to the migratory patterns of birds, to the population count of fish, to the rising and falling of the stock market—the ebb and flow of these events are more or less predictable oscillating systems. They go through cycles. With a little research, we can make reasonably successful guesses about what they're going to do next.

But we rarely guess exactly right. There's always a margin of error. And in these fuzzy spaces in between the certainties, some scientists are finding entirely new patterns, some of which mirror the originals and some of which seem to be their own new universes.

4. No, Really, Is It a Joke?

Well, of course it is. If it wasn't a joke, it wouldn't be true, would it? See point #2.

5. Modern Discordianism

Much of today's Discordianism can be traced to the appearance of the *Principia Discordia* in 1965, a strange little book by Malaclypse the Younger and Lord Omar Khayyam Ravenhurst. I won't attempt to summarize it all here; even if I could, that would just ruin the effect.

You'll just have to go and read it for yourself. Even so, Discordians aren't limited to its teachings—nay, they're expected to make up their own things.

As a group (ha!), we tend to enjoy conspiracy theories, weird science, offbeat philosophy, avant-garde art and literature, and other bits of nonconformity. (No, not the kind of nonconformity that you can buy at that punk rock store at the mall.) Discordianism isn't about doing exactly the opposite of the prevailing order. This isn't nonconformity for its own sake, and it's not nonconformity with a sociopolitical agenda, and it's not the nonconformity that only wants to freak out its parents. I'm talking about the really deeply fringe stuff: the stuff on the cutting edge of edges that people didn't even realize were being cut. The stuff that's SO WEIRD THAT IT DOESN'T EVEN KNOW HOW WEIRD IT IS, AND IT'S NOT EVEN TRYING.

Discordian Magic

How does one even begin to learn Discordian magic? Maybe it seems very advanced and intimidating, and certainly some aspects of it are. However, there is no starting place I can think of that allows you to get "just a little bit of Discordia" and then go on with what you were doing before. Once you step offshore, there's a huge drop-off, and after that it's all deep end. If you see a little bit of it—really see it—it's one of those things you can never unlearn.

Luckily, your survival instincts will kick in and you probably won't drown; you'll just get better at swimming. (Those who can't see it at all are the ones who would drown, but that's okay because they'll never be able to get off the beach anyway.) By the time you feel like you can call yourself an expert, you'll be so far from shore that you may as well just start building your own island, and at that point, you'll be able to do so.

You'll find lots of spells and rituals that purport to be Discordian, but a lot of the basic work will already be familiar. Anyone can always learn something and get fresh ideas from any new source, but the experienced, well-read mage will probably recognize many of the applied-magic techniques in any Discordian magical handbook.

You can probably guess by now that there are no set-in-stone rules for Discordian magic. I have found that the most potent magical applications of Discord tend to happen spontaneously. One must be receptive to weird coincidences, odd connections, and sudden opportunities—the more you acknowledge these events and make use of the currents as they come, the more the universe will provide them.

> **I have found that the most potent magical applications of Discord tend to happen spontaneously. One must be receptive to weird coincidences, odd connections, and sudden opportunities—the more you acknowledge these events and make use of the currents as they come, the more the universe will provide them.**

One's experience and expectations actually create one's reality—this is the wave/particle duality paradox, the proven-in-the-lab quantum physics trick whereby simply looking for a particular condition collapses the wave function in favor of that condition. We tend to see what we expect to see. Discordianism is a way of uncollapsing wave functions. When a being is truly surprised, confused, and

uncertain, there's a moment in which many different realities exist in a number of superimposed states.

If you're engrossed in your studies and you hear a sudden, strange noise behind you, there is an instant in which your settled, predictable reality is upset and that noise could literally be anything. You don't know what to expect, so your reality doesn't know what to create. The noise exists in that state of confusion and quantum superposition until you turn around and collapse the wave function by observing the source, causing many possibilities to settle into one state.

You could argue that the wave function was already collapsed because the thing that made the noise already existed behind you, and that's true. But that leads us down one of those infinite paths of nested realities—the cat in Schrödinger's box certainly observes its own state, collapsing its own wave function, but not that of Schrödinger, who doesn't know if he'll find a live cat or a dead one until he opens the box. When Schrödinger opens the box and sees for himself (and until he does, the cat is still both alive and dead in his reality, regardless of its state in its own original reality—see how the universes split up?), there are still people outside of the laboratory waiting to hear the results. Until Schrödinger comes out and tells them what he saw, the cat still exists in multiple states in their universes. And on and on and so forth to infinity, at which point nobody knows anything about anything anymore.

You can begin to see why humor is such a popular element of Discordia. We fight madness with madness.

But I Digress

…all of which brings us back to Discordia and chaos magic. All of these silly antics and random spewings are designed to surprise, confuse, and keep parts of the consciousness, and thus some realities, in a constant state of flux. If the wave function can be kept from collapsing, or can be brought from stability back to an undefined state, one can actually use that moment of confusion to shift and redefine realities.

The more one lives within this flux, the more one can pretty much reach into the aether and steer reality (i.e., do magic) in new directions. Fine-tuning takes a lot of practice and conditioning, but it can be done, though it's never totally predictable (and a lot of times, the results are better if you don't try to push too hard for anything too specific).

The best advice I can think of for those who wish to explore a Discordian path is: MAKE IT UP YOURSELF. ALL OF IT.

The references I've listed at the end of this article are great starts. There's a reason why they're classics. Read them and get ideas, and then thumb your nose at them. Don't make the mistake of thinking

they're the absolute definition of Discordianism. THEY'RE NOT THE BOSS OF YOU.

Here are some exercises:

Think about your reality. Not the one that the marketers and the newscasters and the teachers and the textbooks and the Mystical Authorities are trying to shove into your cranium. Your reality. What is your universe like? How do you know it's yours and not your idea of someone else's idea of what your ideas should be?

Are you there now? If not, why not?

Prepare and cast a spell to make some small corner of the external world (such as it is) conform more to YOUR world. Use Discordian principles (surprise, confusion, nonsense, humor, pudding, etc.) and maybe try some techniques and ideas that you find in your research.

Now, try it again, but this time, don't prepare anything. Just set the idea in a corner of your mind and go about your day, and see what may present itself to you. Pay attention to fuzzy "in-between" feelings and those little clicking sounds. Respond spontaneously. Follow impulses without thinking about how other people—or yourself—are going to judge you for it. (Give your common sense permission to cast the deciding vote, though. This isn't about taking dangerous risks just because an idea suddenly jumped into your head.)

Which way worked better for you? Everyone's results will vary.

Fnord

I can't speak for any other Discordians, but if I had to come up with a reason why I chose this path, I'd say that it's about keeping things moving and changing. It's about discovery, destruction, and creation, and how they're really all the same thing. It's about recognizing the need for both order and chaos, developing a sense of balance between them, and keeping everything in existence from sinking back down into the horror of that static perfection where nothing ever changes and no one exists except the One because it was really awful and lonely there and that's how We went mad and why We became Many in the first place.

It's all an illusion, but it's a darned good one.

FURTHER READING

Principia Discordia by Malaclypse the Younger and Lord Omar Khayyam Ravenhurst.

Anything by Robert Anton Wilson, particularly *The Illuminatus! Trilogy*.

The Book of the SubGenius (and the two sequels, and anything else involving Ivan Stang & friends).

Anything by Peter Carroll, particularly *Liber Kaos*.

Chaos: Making a New Science by James Gleick.

Jymi x/ø ("Reverend Variable") *has been practicing all kinds of magic for years and years and still finds itself with very little certainty about how or why anything works. It holds degrees in English and Digital Media Production, and is currently ignoring its Latin homework in favor of something shiny that it found on the Internet. (Please visit us at www.reverend variable.com.) It has had quite enough of the "normal" world, preferring instead to spend its days studying, writing, arting, and developing interactive storytelling websites based on a series of dreams and the many adventures that it has with its friends from several other dimensions. In its spare time, it tentaryardle blargh wumba eeg skrrrg gritz yikkity blergh and rearranging furniture.*

Illustrator: Jennifer Hewitson

The Path of a Priestess

Stephanie Woodfield

Priestess. It's a word that invokes images of ancient ceremonies, of sibyls proclaiming prophecies, and of women of power speaking for, honoring, and making offerings to the old gods. From the women shamans of Siberia to the Tawananna priestess queens of the Hittites, women have filled roles of spiritual power throughout time.

When I am asked to describe my spiritual path, there are several words that come to mind. I am a Pagan, a polytheist, a Witch, and a priestess. Certainly I am a Witch: I practice magick and divination and do ritual and healing work. I am a polytheist: I see the gods as vital living forces, individuals with identities and distinct personalities, tastes, and mannerisms; and recognizing and respecting this colors my practices and interaction with them. And then there is the word "priestess." Like the word "Witch," this term means different things to different people, sometimes vastly different things. But of all the terms I use to describe my spiritual path, "priestess" is the most personal one, the one that holds the most weight and meaning for me. A priestess is not only what I am, but the term that brings all the others together, a title that describes the practices that are at the heart of my devotion to the gods.

But what exactly is a priestess? What it means to be a priestess varies from person to person and from tradition to tradition. In ancient cultures, it most likely meant one was dedicated to a specific god or goddess, and was possibly serving or living in a temple. In some

cases, priestesses served both a religious and a political function, the assumption being a leader needed both the advice of the gods and their favor to rule successfully. The Tawananna priestesses were the lifelong consorts to the Hittite kings. Each Tawananna priestess was seen as the physical embodiment of the sun goddess, but also ruled when the king was away in battle. In Delphi, the Pythia was the most prestigious and authoritative oracle among the Greeks. The prophecies this priestess spoke were sought by kings and commoners alike. In tribal cultures, we find women shamans who, like their male counterparts, acted as bridges between the mortal realm and the realm of spirits. Although priestesses fill different roles in their cultures, in general the function of a priestess remains the same: serving a particular deity and acting as a bridge between the divine and the community, whether through ritual, prophecy, or making offerings on the community's behalf.

To modern Pagans, the word "priestess" most likely brings to mind the drawing down the moon ritual or esbats and sabbats led by the local coven's High Priestess. In general, there is a tendency in the Pagan community to consider anyone who leads a ritual or coven to be a priest or priestess, or these titles become another level to achieve within a tradition. But while part of the role of a priesthood is to do ritual work, this is not the defining function of a priest or priestess. I have never seen the function of a priestess as just that of leading rituals, or as simply another degree within a group, nor do I think every Pagan needs to take up the mantle of priesthood. It is not a path for everyone.

My own path as a priestess is deeply rooted in my devotion to the Morrigan. I work with several deities and have built strong relationships with them. I have felt Brighid's fiery inspiration move through me, walked the shadowed paths of the otherworlds with Cernunnos, and am often reminded by the Dagda not to take myself so seriously.

These gods are familiar to me, a vital part of my life, but still I am not their priestess. That dedication and devotion belongs to the Morrigan, and goes deeper than the rest. And perhaps this is why we have so many varied definitions of a priestess. A priestess of Bast would be drawn to doing very different work in the world than would, say, a priestess of Artemis or Brighid.

The call of the Morrigan has led me down many paths. The Morrigan has become an inseparable part of myself; she is my patron, my mother, my goddess. For many years I worked with her only as my patron before dedicating myself to her as a priestess. At first I thought that dedicating myself to the Morrigan as my patron deity and being her priestess were the same thing, but one can be dedicated to a god or goddess or work with them as a patron and choose not to take up the path of a priesthood.

Dedicating yourself to a deity is about your personal relationship with them; becoming a priest or priestess of a deity takes that devotion a step further. A priestess serves the gods, her community, and those around her. When we build a deep connection with a deity, we fulfill both our own spiritual needs and those of the people around us. The priestess becomes a vessel for the energies of the gods to come into the world. It is amazing what we can accomplish for ourselves and others when we open ourselves to the divine. Letting the energies of a deity

> **Dedicating yourself to a deity is about your personal relationship with them; becoming a priest or priestess of a deity takes that devotion a step further. A priestess serves the gods, her community, and those around her.**

move through you and doing their work in the world isn't always something that happens in ritual. Sometimes bringing their energy into the world may happen in unexpected ways.

Shortly after I did my priestess dedication ritual, my mother was diagnosed with cancer. My brother and I would alternate bringing her to the hospital for chemo. Those days were filled with hours spent sitting in waiting rooms and listening to doctors explaining test results. It was the last place I expected to do the work of a priestess, but the Morrigan had different plans. One day when I was sitting in the waiting room while my mother was receiving her chemo treatment, I felt an overwhelming need to be moving. It was almost like when you leave the house and have forgotten to turn a light off—an anxiousness in the back of my mind was telling me there was something I needed to do, only I didn't know what it was. It came out of nowhere. I was calm one minute, then the feeling filled me. I couldn't sit still, so I got up and started walking. I didn't really pay attention to where I was going; I just followed the feeling.

Then finally, when I walked past an open door, the feeling was gone—just like that, like a rug had been pulled out from under me. It startled me. I almost felt like I was going to fall, and put my hands in front of me as if to brace myself. From inside the room, an amused woman's voice asked me if I was lost. And that is how I met Rose, a woman in her eighties who was dying of pancreatic cancer. I sat and talked to her for over an hour, and from then on, when I brought my mother in for her treatments, I would visit with Rose. Other times, both my mother and I would sit with Rose, and she would tell us about her life and we would tell her about ours. Rose's remaining family members lived on the other side of the country, so she rarely had visitors. She accepted that she was dying with grace and even humor, but my heart ached that there was no one to be with her through this process, to hear her stories, to listen to the wisdom she wished to pass one. There was no one to act as a midwife from this life to the next.

Rose wasn't a Pagan, and we never even spoke about religion. But talking with her and listening to her talk about her life became a way to celebrate a life well lived, and one that was coming to an end. I wasn't in ritual garb and I wasn't speaking invocations to the gods, but nonetheless I felt the Morrigan beside me. This was part of the work she needed me to do. It served her, and filled the needs of a dying woman, who I am sure had no clue who the Morrigan was. But all the same, the goddess led me to the exact right place I needed to be, and placed the work I needed to do before me. When Rose passed, I lit a candle on the Morrigan's altar. I made offerings and did ritual work asking that Rose's spirit safely pass beyond the veil, and celebrated her life in my own way.

Given the Morrigan's connection to death and liminal space, it is not so surprising that she would lead me to help someone who was passing from this life to the next. But it was not the kind of work I expected her to guide me to do when I first decided to dedicate myself to this path. As a priestess, I lead rituals, I teach, and I honor the gods. But the lesson I learned from Rose is that the work the gods call us to do isn't always within a ritual circle.

At heart, a priestess serves as an intermediary between the gods and the community. But we no longer live in tribal cultures or in small, isolated communities. Our tribe is the greater world now. My work as a priestess may involve facilitating a ritual for a group one day and passing on a divinely inspired message to someone I just met in my everyday life the next. It might be offering a shoulder to cry on to a coworker. It might be found in the peace that comes from small, simple acts of devotion, of leaving offerings on the Morrigan's altar each morning. Or it could be lighting a candle and simply talking to the Morrigan, and learning to listen to her voice in the cries of crows overhead or in the stillness of my own heart. Letting the energies of a deity move through you and doing their work in the world isn't always something that happens in ritual. Sometimes bringing their energy into the world may happen in unexpected ways.

Stephanie Woodfield *is the author of* Celtic Lore and Spellcraft of the Dark Goddess: Invoking the Morrigan *and* Drawing Down the Sun: Rekindle the Magick of the Solar Goddesses. *Stephanie has been a practicing Witch and Priestess of the Morrigan for over sixteen years. Her articles have appeared in* SageWoman *magazine,* The Portal, *and on the* Witches' Voice *website. She is one of the founding members of* Morrigu's Daughters, *an online sisterhood dedicated to the Morrigan. You can find her on her blog,* Dark Goddess Musings, *at* http://darkgoddessmusings.blogspot.com.

Illustrator: Tim Foley

Witchy Living

DAY-BY-DAY WITCHCRAFT

What to Do When Your Magick Doesn't Work

Cassius Sparrow

Eventually we will all go through it. Something happens, whether it's gradual or all at once, and the magick just seems to stop working. For some of us, this is a terrifying experience: it brings up a lot of self-doubt and the burning question of *what am I doing wrong?* This is a good time to take a step back and look at your methods and your situation to see where some changes need to be made.

There are different reasons why magick stops working for someone. Sometimes the problem is with your emotional and physical state of mind, sometimes it's the environment you are working in, and sometimes it's the spell itself. The important thing to remember is that this is only temporary, and the solutions to all of these problems are simpler than you might think.

Overcoming the Self

The most common reason a spell may not work is that you may not be in the right place for it, physically, emotionally, or even both. Have you been going through periods of extreme stress lately?

Stress is the number one reason why spells seem to fizzle and die. This, unfortunately, only adds more stress to an already frazzled Witch, leading to a vicious cycle that is sometimes difficult to break.

Stress is the number one reason why spells seem to fizzle and die. This, unfortunately, only adds more stress to an already frazzled Witch, leading to a vicious cycle that is sometimes difficult to break. This is the best time to take a step back from your magickal workings, take a deep breath, reevaluate your situation, and ask yourself some questions: Is the process of this spell causing you more stress? Will it accomplish an immediate goal that will relieve your stress, or is it only going to exacerbate the situation? It could be a spell you have worked a thousand times before, but if you are emotionally and physically drained, then it simply isn't going to work.

Take this opportunity to breathe and re-ground yourself. Remind yourself that roadblocks like these are only temporary bumps in your spiritual journey, and, like all things, these too shall pass. Immerse

yourself in an environment that makes you feel most at ease. Go for a long walk and commune with nature. Pamper yourself with a nice, hot bath featuring your favorite essential oils. Pop in a videogame and take out your frustrations on clusters of pixels. Whatever your favorite method of relaxation is, use it as a time to meditate on what changes need to be made. Perhaps you need a break from your magickal workings. If you take a few days to recharge your spiritual energies before trying again, and approach the situation with a fresh mind and spirit, you might find that the old spark has come right back.

But what if it's been a while since you flexed your magickal fingers and tried any spellcrafting? Maybe there is a fine layer of spiritual "dust" that has settled over you that you need to shake off. A simple shower won't be enough to clean off that sort of muck; you will need a thorough self-cleansing. The most common forms of self-cleansing are through incense smoke or ritual bath. If you already have a preferred method for self-cleansing, use that, but amplify its cleansing and restorative properties by adding appropriate herbs, powders, and oils to the usual mix.

If you are going the smoke-cleansing route, powdered dragon's blood resin, frankincense, sea salt, white sage, sweetgrass, and lavender are all powerful cleansing agents. Try a mixture of them, or add one or two to your usual routine. If you use white sage, try to find locally grown and sustainably sourced white sage. Burn the herbs and powders while wafting the smoke over you, starting with your feet and slowly moving up your body to the top of your head. Breathe deeply, shedding your spiritual muck, and draw into yourself clean air, the freeing feeling of starting fresh. Affirm to yourself—aloud— that you *can* do this. Give yourself a good shake, unsettle that "dust," flex your fingers, and wiggle your toes. Stretch, smile, and try again.

If a bath appeals more to you, add essentials oils of lavender, sage, or frankincense while the water is running, or dissolve sea salt infused with these oils in the water. You can add powdered dragon's blood to the water, but be aware that it may leave a red stain both on your skin and in your bathtub, so do so with care and be prepared to scrub! Rose water is a popular addition to many beauty routines, and with good reason: it is a gentle, natural cleanser that is good for the skin, and what's good for your skin can also be good for the spirit. Add rose water to your bath, float white rose petals in the water, or, for a double punch, use both. Burn white candles around your bathtub (but be sure to be mindful of fire safety!) to provide some ambiance. Submerge yourself completely, allowing the water to wash away your cares and the grime that is holding you back. Gently exfoliate your skin, using the rose water if you decided to incorporate it into your bath. Breathe deeply, and, as with the smoke cleansing, affirm aloud that this magickal hiccup shall pass, that you are shedding this like-dead skin, and that when you emerge, you will be ready to start fresh.

Regardless of the reasons that prompted it, a good spiritual self-cleansing can help any Witch who has felt his or her magickal workings fizzle or fade.

Refreshing Your Surroundings

So you've done it: you've cleansed your body and spirit and shaken the devils off your back, and now you're ready to launch yourself back into the action. You've found the perfect spell, gathered everything you needed, and yet…*still nothing!* Now what? Before you begin to panic, take a look at your surroundings and examine where you are trying to do your work. Has negativity been brought into that space recently? Does the air feel stale, tired, or uneasy? Have you been neglecting the upkeep of your altar or shrines? Think of it as "spring cleaning." Whatever the season, a good, thorough cleaning may be in order: out with the old atmosphere and in with the new!

Open the windows and let some fresh air in to start. If the area has a door that opens to the outside, open that as well. Stand in the center of the space and take a good look around yourself, making a list of the areas that need attention first. Dusty altar or shrines? Let those be the first on  your list. Clean the area around them, as well as above or underneath. Burn some incense while you clean, if you'd like, letting the smoke waft around the room as a passive cleaner. Hum, whistle, or sing to yourself as you work, or play music to lift your energies and stir up the energy in the room. Try to avoid harsh, chemical-laden cleaners, and make your own by combining rose water and fresh spring water and dissolving a pinch of sea salt in the mixture. Use a fresh sponge or cleaning cloth, and discard it when you're finished. Take care to clean the thresholds in the room as well, such as doorways and windowsills. If the room is carpeted, vacuum thoroughly and immediately change the bag or empty the canister. For hardwood or tile floors, start at the corners farthest from the entrance and sweep toward the door, sweeping the negativity and the stagnation out the door with the dust pile. You can purchase a new, cheap broom for this, or if you are a crafty Witch, make one. Feel free to use your homemade cleaner to mop the floors.

Take the time to clean your magickal tools as well. Organize them neatly, either on your altar or within whatever storage space you have for them. Can you remember the last time you replaced some of your oils and stones? This may a good time to take an inventory of what you have and what you need to replace. When in doubt, toss it out! Oils that have become discolored or whose scents have changed or faded are in need of replacement.

When you're finished cleaning, return to the center of the room. If you'd like to play music, find something fast and upbeat. Sing along, dance, spin, ring bells—ultimately, you want to stir the energy within yourself and channel it into the area, lifting your own spirits and also saturating the very foundation of the room with these energies.

Then stop for a moment and take another good look at the area. Attend to any spots still in need of cleaning that you might have missed on the first go-round, then feel out the atmosphere. Does it feel more energized? Is the air less stale? Make a reminder to yourself to maintain the upkeep of your working space, and repeat this ritual regularly to keep the creative energies flowing in the room.

Sourcing Spells

Occasionally, the reason a spell isn't working has nothing to do with the Witch or the environment. Sometimes it lies within the spell itself. Spellcrafting is a fluid science, and we learn new things about it every day. So while you cannot be a walking, breathing encyclopedia of all things magickal, a little research never hurt anyone. What is the source of your spell? Did you hear about it from a friend who has this friend who tried it and it *totally* worked for them? Did you find it on a rarely updated—and probably abandoned—website and thought it looked interesting? Take some time to research the spell and everything it entails. Talk to your fellow Witches and ask for their feedback. Have they tried it? If so, did it work for them? Did they need to make changes to it? Use this information to make appropriate changes, or just abandon the spell entirely and start over with a different one.

The most important thing to realize during this experience is that magickal hiccups happen, but they are easily conquered. Patience, self-reflection, and an open mind will be your most valuable tools while you assess your current situation and take the steps necessary to get yourself back on track. View it as a learning opportunity that will only help you grow and mature. Remain calm, stay positive, and remember: this shall pass.

Cassius Sparrow *is a Hellenic Polytheist, Witch, tarot reader, and author. He is a devotee of Hermes and has been a practicing Pagan for over ten years. He currently lives on the Gulf Coast of Florida with his darling wife and their cat, Zucca. In his free time, he can be found writing, baking, or working in his herb garden. Contact him at cassiussparrow@gmail.com.*

Illustrator: Kathleen Edwards

We Are Everywhere: Finding Pagans in the Wild

Laurel Reufner

Have you ever taken a good look around and wondered where all of the other Pagans are hiding? Books and other statistics often tell us that folks on an Earth-centered path are found in all walks of life, working in a vast variety of jobs and careers, but actually encountering them outside of Pagan events can be challenging. However, it can also be quite rewarding, affirming that, once the circle opens, we aren't alone in the big world.

If you pay attention and notice the details about the people around you, it's amazing what you can uncover.

Spotting spiritual travelers is a skill that only gets better with practice, and there are some details that make it easier to do. Let's take a look at some of them.

I used to be much, much better at paying attention to what was happening in the larger area around me, but having had children seems to have narrowed my vision somewhat. I've been trying to get better about it now that my daughters are in their teens and I no longer have to stay focused solely on what they're about to get into. In doing so, I began to notice signs of Paganism everywhere. It gave me quite a warm and cozy feeling to discover that Athens County, Ohio, was home to many more Earth-centered practitioners than just the ones I'd already met at our local Unitarian Universalist Fellowship. Over the course of the last few years, I've learned that there are some particular things to look for when trying to find other Pagans.

Of course, it was a piece of lovely jewelry that started my "Pagans in the wild" journey. Actually, jewelry figures in many of my encounters, simply because we Pagans often wear pieces of it, whether as mere adornment, as a show of our spiritual inclinations, or as an amulet or talisman of some sort. In this case, it was a beautiful piece of fine jewelry made of silver and semiprecious stones, done in a triple-moon design. I think the middle stone was an aquamarine or blue topaz. It

 was gorgeous and it was being worn by a cashier at our local Walmart. Sadly, I was too shy to comment on it the first time, but the second time I found myself in her line, I couldn't resist the urge to pipe up and compliment her. Turns out the piece was an original, and it was indeed what I thought it was. We both smiled

in recognition of shared knowledge, enjoyed a few more moments of conversation, and went on about our respective tasks.

I don't know about the cashier, but I was thrilled to have met another Pagan out in real life, to have made contact with someone who shared similar spiritual beliefs to mine. Encouraged, I started keeping my eyes open for more. Another encounter occurred with the attendant at a local dry cleaners. The giveaway this time was an obvious silver pentagram ring. We had a lovely chat about how Pagans are far more prevalent in Athens than either of us had previously thought.

So, the first takeaway here is to remember to look at the jewelry folks are wearing whenever you're out shopping and running errands. Wearing lots of silver jewelry, especially rings and bracelets, is a good indication, but sometimes just a single, simple item with some sort of Earth-centered spiritual symbolism will get the message across.

Remember that it works both ways, though, and consider making yourself more visible to others in your area as well. You never know when another Pagan might cross your path. If you're not comfortable being fully out of the broom closet, try something subtle that only others Pagans will recognize, such a Thor's hammer, Celtic knotwork (although Celtic designs are also common with non-Pagans), or a subtle goddess symbol.

I have a small pair of silver goddess earrings that often earn compliments, but I'm also in a position where I can proudly wear goddess pendants or even my pentagram and not worry about a backlash. Assess your own situation and comfort level and act accordingly. Who knows what might come of it?

Do you belong to any special interest groups? Don't be surprised if there are other Pagans in your midst. After all, we all have lives outside of our groves, circles, and covens. Start paying better attention to your fellow group members and see if you notice any indications. Books, jewelry, clothing, or even verbal references could indicate a kindred spirit.

A good case in point is our local region for National Novel Writing Month (NaNoWriMo). It turns out that nearly half of the most active folks are Pagan. The giveaway that started it all? Yep, you guessed it—a piece of jewelry. Another writer showed up during my first year as municipal liaison wearing a beautiful pentagram ring, which I noticed right away. I'm embarrassed to confess that I never commented on it during the first NaNoWriMo that we spent writing together, but I'm glad I did the second time. We've since become good friends, and our conversations at write-ins have helped some others feel free to join in.

Once again, it's helpful to have something that identifies you to those in the know, be it a piece of jewelry, an article of clothing, or even a book or periodical. Being able to comment on something another person is wearing gives both parties a chance to start a conversation, even if it doesn't go any further than that particular encounter.

Finally, my favorite stories about meeting Pagans out in non-Pagan settings involve people who were already my friends. My good, long-term friends already know about my chosen spiritual path, but since it's not really a topic for everyday conversation, some of my newer friends haven't learned of it yet.

> It's helpful to have something that identifies you to those in the know, be it a piece of jewelry, an article of clothing, or even a book or periodical. Being able to comment on something another person is wearing gives both parties a chance to start a conversation, even if it doesn't go any further than that particular encounter.

We had some new friends over for dinner one day, and the wife stepped into the kitchen area so we could talk more easily while I finished something up. Turning to read the magnet collection on the side of the fridge, she noticed my "Get a Taste of Religion, Lick a Witch" bumper sticker, which I'd turned into a magnet. Curious, she asked if I was Pagan. When I smiled and nodded, she smiled back and told me that she was as well. Needless to say, the conversation took a turn in the direction of religion. It was interesting talking about how we'd both wound up on an Earth-centered path in spite of our Christian upbringings. We also had a good laugh, since not only had we already known each other for a few months by that point, but she'd also been in my home—including the kitchen—several times. She'd just never turned to look at the refrigerator before.

A year or so later, while hosting a different group of people, that witchy friend and I discovered that the third woman in the group was also a Pagan, following a druidic path. Bet you'll never guess the giveaway. Yep, she was wearing a gorgeous tree of life pendant. It was nice to have a friend with firsthand knowledge of that particular path. You never know when you might have questions.

My final anecdote involves a good, open-minded friend who is not Pagan. I work as a part-time volunteer for her in one of the area schools. She was extra excited to see me one day, dragging me off to meet another school employee who also turned out to be Pagan.

So, my fellow Pagans include a Walmart cashier, a dry cleaning attendant, a scriptwriter and college instructor, a writer and college instructor, a college student, a retired Marine and accountant, a social worker, and a bank teller. I also know an archaeology professor, a sociology professor, a librarian, a former lawyer turned college professor, and at least two school teachers, although I met all of them at a more traditional Pagan gathering. An interesting cross-section of our population is featured on this list.

Pagans are in all walks of life, working all sorts of jobs. Some of them may even be your friend already. All you need to do is make yourself more open to interacting with strangers and then start noticing the details about them. Look at their jewelry, and pay attention to how they're dressed and how they talk. If you're lucky enough to be invited into their home, take a quick look around and see if there are any other signs that an Earth-centered spiritualist might live there. Just please, don't be obvious and stare. Trust me, that's not going to get you where you want to go. Being friendly, open-minded, and approachable is good; coming off like a creepy stalker isn't.

Finally, make yourself identifiable to others who are also looking for like-minded folks. Wear some jewelry that says you might be Pagan. It doesn't even have to be anything as overt as a pentacle dangling from your neck. If you can, show a peek of that spiritual tattoo hiding on your shoulder. Use the phrase "Blessed be" or "Thank the gods."

That last one especially is subtle enough that most folks won't even catch it. Set out a Bast statue in your living room. It's all about being willing to put yourself out there a wee bit so that others can connect with you.

While it's true that I currently live in a liberal arts college town (Ohio University, anyone?) where it's much easier to find folks from all different walks of life, I really do believe that you can connect with Earth-centered folks just about anywhere. I'm still trying to meet some in the wilds of my hometown—I haven't given up yet. I know that they are there. We just haven't connected yet.

Laurel Reufner's *mother can verify that she grew up a "wild child" in farming country. Laurel has been Earth-centered for around a quarter century and really enjoys writing about whatever topics grab her attention. She has always lived in southeastern Ohio and currently calls Athens County home, where she lives with her wonderful husband and two wild daughters of her own. Find her online at* Laurel Reufner's Lair, *http://laurelreufner.blogspot.com, or on Facebook.*

Illustrator: Bri Hermanson

Why Is Journaling Such an Angsty Process for So Many People?

Susan Pesznecker

Journaling is something we magickal people are told is important. We're encouraged to journal every day. We're told how meaningful journaling should be. We begin with gorgeous journals or fancy digital tablets and always with the best of intentions, but all too often, and despite meaning well, our journaling efforts fade away. I can't tell you how many people I've talked to who say, "You know, I tried it, and I didn't like it," or "I journaled for a few days, and then I just kind of stopped," or "I didn't see what good it was doing."

Here's the thing: If you work with spiritual paths, deities, tools, natural forces, or other magickal mojo, there's an immense amount of "good" that journaling can do you. Even better, it can become a re-warding, soul-enriching, joyful (dare I say fun?) practice. The key is understanding why journaling works, its benefits, and how to make it work for you.

The Scientific Lowdown: How Does Writing Affect Our Brains?

Let's begin by considering writing and the brain.

When you write by hand, you stimulate a collection of cells in the base of your brain—the reticular activating system. This filters the incoming information and causes your brain to pay close attention to whatever you're writing about. The *physical act* of writing—of holding a pen or pencil and writing letters on paper—triggers this response and activates your brain's frontal and parietal lobes, which are associated with speaking, writing, reasoning, problem solving, and the interpretation of language and words. When you write, these parts of your brain become more active. Your senses heighten and you become more alert and aware of your surroundings and of the memories you're activating through your writing. Simply said, writing switches your brain to the ON position.

Writing digitally (i.e., typing on a keyboard or keypad) has similar effects to handwriting, but research shows clearly that brain activity is significantly stronger in response to handwriting than to digital writing. Given that handwriting is rapidly disappearing from our culture—here in the U.S., electronic signatures are now widely accepted in commerce, correspondence is exclusively typewritten, and many schoolchildren are no longer being taught to write in cursive—this is an interesting and significant finding.

The act of writing also activates a "story response." When we listen to someone explain something or when we watch an informative video or a Prezi or PowerPoint presentation, specific areas of our brains are stimulated to process the sounds and images and turn them into understandable language. We watch, we listen, and we under-
stand. That's valuable, but that's also as far as it goes.

In contrast, when we watch or listen to a *story*—a narrative style with a beginning, middle, and end that also carries symbolic meaning—our motor cortex is activated just as if we were *in* the story as active participants, actually experiencing the sights, sounds, and actions being shared in the story. Different parts of the brain activate, our breathing and heart rate pick up a little, and we respond physically to the storytelling. Studies have shown that the listener's brain activity actually falls into sync with the storyteller's. A similar process happens when we journal: the brain perceives that this is a kind of personal storytelling, and the brain is fully activated and engaged, not only making the undertaking more interesting but also involving us fully in the scene being described. In this way, journaling helps a writer access deep memories, and also helps to encode new, fresh memories for later retrieval.

Another exciting finding is that the physiological effects of journaling mimic those of meditation. When we journal, respiration and heart rate slow, muscles relax, stress ebbs away, and the brain slips into a zone of heightened awareness and recall. Time seems to become fluid, as when, during a journaling or writing session, the writer looks up to find that an hour has mysteriously slipped by—instead of the ten to fifteen minutes she thought had passed. Stream-of-consciousness-style journaling relieves stress and alters the brain wave patterns, and writing in journals and diaries has also been shown to slow activity in the brain's amygdala, which reduces stress and stress-related reactions.

What does all of this mean, and why is it important? It reveals that writing can directly influence our brain activity, providing cognitive benefits. It suggests that journaling has effects similar to those of effective meditation. It shows that journaling is a valuable means of helping us understand and remember, and that it may reduce stress and instill a sense of peace—useful effects in today's crazy world.

All About Writing

Let's consider writing itself. Writing is a kind of symbolic language—a way of using symbols (letters, images, signs) to stand in for or represent words. Until writing was invented, all communication was oral, and knowledge and history were transmitted through speech. With the creation of alphabets and writing tools, history could finally be preserved in a concrete form.

Historic evidence suggests that as soon as people began writing, they also began keeping journals and records, which served important roles in human history and exploration. When a ship set out across the ocean, its ship's log or captain's log was its most valuable possession and the log keeper the most valuable crewmember, second only to the captain. Without the journal, much of the journey's importance would have been lost. The value of these records persists today, although they're more likely to be in digital format.

In the same way that an explorer's journal marked and recorded adventures, a magickal journal can help you track your own journey. You'll be able to chart your discoveries, successes, and even the

occasional snafu. You'll record and later recall a ritual or holiday or blessing that worked well, and you'll be able to tweak it for repeat use. You'll note important dates and detail those aha moments of gnosis dear to the hearts of magick users. Journaling can help develop your memory and make you a participant in your own storytelling, bringing your words and feelings to life. And by noting details such as date, weather, moon phase, or astrological cycle, you'll make connections between your own observations and natural occurrences.

Also, you may choose to join a group of people who share a spiritual tradition—e.g., a grove, circle, or coven—or you may already be a member. In many groups, magickal tomes are important parts of practice and training. The writing you do now may prove to be an important part of your spiritual future. Experimenting with and personalizing the journaling process can bring your inner muse to life and inspire your magickal processes. And consider this: The act of using letters and pictures on paper (or screen) to lay down ideas, thoughts, rituals, spells, and experiences? Encoding reality into symbolic language? Sounds like magick to me!

Selecting a Journal: Digital or Handwritten?

As we discussed earlier, there are known neuroscientific benefits to writing by hand. Doing so integrates visual, motor, and cognitive functions, supports learning and memory, and makes the writing process more fun. Using a 3-D journal requires only you and some inexpensive tools, and if you want to bring artistry into your journaling, it's easy to cut, paste, illuminate, and sketch ad lib.

But we are living in the digital age, and many people are most comfortable doing their writing on a digital device. There are definite advantages to digital journaling, specifically in the ability to save every word easily and to search for and locate entries by date or key word. Digital files can be backed up, protecting them against loss or damage. Working directly with artistic techniques is still possible with a digital journal, although it's trickier (much more of a learning curve) and limits the possibilities.

Choose a method of journaling that is easy and satisfying for you. If it's easy to use, you'll be more likely to use it often and to reap benefits from doing so. If using a digital journal will make your process work better, by all means do so.

If taking a handwritten approach, you might start with a lined notebook or a loose-leaf binder, the latter allowing you to add and rearrange pages. If you choose a paper journal, I suggest one made from archival-quality paper. Archival paper has a low acid content and will last hundreds of years without fading or deteriorating. It costs more than regular paper, but it's worth the price. Archival inks and adhesives are available, too.

If using a digital journal, you'll likely be considering a desk-style computer, laptop, or tablet. I recommend choosing the largest screen and keyboard available. I cannot recommend using a smartphone for journaling—the keypad and screen are so small that these restrictions will directly affect your process. As I tell my college writing students, writing an essay (or journal entry) on a smart phone is like trying to cook Thanksgiving dinner on a one-burner backpacking stove!

Ideally, your journal should be big enough to use comfortably but small enough to keep close for quick access. It may be hard- or soft-backed; hard-backed journals hold up longer than soft ones. Nowa-

days it's easy to find journals with beautifully decorative covers, including those matching an area of magickal interest, a spirit animal or totem, or some other meaningful symbol. Many elegant leather- or wood-bound journals are refillable, allowing the journal to become perpetual.

Many folks choose a two-journal system. They carry a small "scratch" journal or field book for everyday notes, expanding or recopying significant passages into a more formal volume or a digital file. Or they might do all of their initial work in digital format and then hand-write important materials into a Book of Shadows or another sacred volume.

The moral of this story is to choose a method that makes sense for you and the kind of journaling process you wish to work with. Whatever your choice, before sinking money into high-end options, I recommend an initial period of experimentation.

Dedicating and Safekeeping

After settling on a journal, many like to formalize the relationship with a ritual of consecration or dedication. After all, you and your journal are entering into a relationship of sorts. Another option is to create a blessing, writing it on the inside of the front cover or at the top of the digital file. Both ritual and blessings might ask that the journal serve as an inspired tool of wisdom, guidance, focus, etc. Here is an example:

As my words
Are added here,
May they inspire
My memories clear.

You'll also want to consider your journal's safekeeping, for a magickal journal is deeply personal. No one should look into your journal without your permission, for doing so not only breaks your own privacy but may affect the magickal nature of the work. When you aren't using your journal, keep it in a safe place so it doesn't fall into others' hands. Digital files can be passcoded. You can wrap a 3-D journal in a special cloth, tying it closed with a piece of cord or ribbon (you'll be surprised at how well a simple knot or set of knots discourages interlopers from peeking). This can become part of a protective ritual, as in:

Guard my words,
And keep them safe,
Here within
This treasured place.

In the same way that some people will keep a new tool, a new Tarot deck, or a new set of runes with them for a period of time so that tool and human can form a bond, you may wish to keep your new journal close for a certain period—one week is always a good marker. This allows you to get to know each another, adding to the potential power of the shared process.

Getting Started

You have a journal ready to go, and you're ready to begin. Now what?

First, start small. By this, I mean don't hold yourself to a daily schedule or demand a specific word count. If you lock yourself into a you-must-do-this-much type of writing early on, it can easily feel overwhelming—like a chore instead of a pleasure—and after all, this process is supposed to be fun, right? Try to journal every day or two, but don't expect a lot. Just write down a few thoughts, ideas, and experiences in whatever way works for you. Start small and let your journaling grow as it wants to.

Second, capture ideas as they occur. Keep a small notebook in your purse, backpack, or computer bag, ready to capture ideas as they occur to you. In Joan Didion's essay "On Keeping a Notebook," she writes about capturing a list of sensory impressions and details. Doing so allows the writer to come back later, read the list, and recall the events, expanding them as a traditional journal entry. This "idea capture" can be a wonderful source of journaling ideas. And trust me: the fleeting, really cool thought you have at 10:00 am will be gone by 5:00 pm if you don't write it down.

Third, your journal doesn't have to be written! We think of journals as involving writing, but you can also journal effectively with drawings, sketches, maps, diagrams, and other visual methods. Try sketching a gorgeous sunrise instead of writing about it. Or supplement written content with art, as in writing the details of a ritual and sketching the altar layout. Often, getting over the it-doesn't-have-to-be-written hurdle is all that's needed to make journaling more fun.

Fourth, allow yourself to write badly at first. As composition theorist Bruce Ballenger explains, this means letting yourself fast-capture ideas and impressions without worrying about making them perfect. By letting yourself brain-dump ideas onto the paper as fast as you can, you open up a creative channel between brain and paper (or screen) and you'll access ideas you never knew were there. As for editing, keep a lid on it (at least at first), for when editing starts, creativity switches off.

What Should I Journal About?

The answer is simple: work with whatever content seems important or relevant to your magickal self or your growth as a person. This might mean appreciating the moonrise, writing about an omen you noticed on your daily walk, creating a new sigil, or writing out a table for a five-year plan. Your journaling—whether written, artsy, or a combination of both—should feel important to you. Adding a date and day to each entry helps with later review, and if you want a bit more structure, mention your mood, the moon phase, weather, zodiac, tides, or other natural markers. Push past "basic" writing and create a story, poem, prayer, charm, or song. Journaling has no limits and no rules.

> **What should you journal about? The answer is simple: work with whatever content seems important or relevant to your magickal self or your growth as a person.**

Going Artsy

Are you curious about exploring a more art-based approach to journaling? You may think, "It sounds fun, but I can't draw!" And I'm here to say, "It doesn't matter!" This is *your* journal, and no one is going to grade your work. The point is to have fun and develop your own journaling process, and if using art materials helps, it's all good.

Rustle up some crayons, colored pencils, gel pens, deckling scissors, pastels, watercolors, or whatever materials make you happy. Begin with a blank page, or look over previous entries and add something artsy to

them. Capture images, sensations, and feelings. Bring in scrapbooking techniques: use special papers, stamps, stickers, photographs, cutouts from maps or pamphlets, pressed plants, samples of earth or stone in tiny glassine envelopes, or anything that appeals to you. Try your hand at ink-making or even making your

own paper—it's easy to find instructions on the Web. For ultra-simple ink, try berry juice, or crumble soot (allow a candle to blacken the back of a spoon) into a drop or two of water.

Illumination is another great technique for art-inspired journaling. In an illuminated manuscript, the text is supplemented by colorful ornamentation, such as decorated initials, borders, calligraphy, or highly detailed drawings, frequently taken from heraldry or religious symbolism. Probably the most famous illuminated manuscript is *The Books of Kells*, dating to AD 800 and residing in the Trinity College Library in Dublin, Ireland. *The Book of Kells* is fully available online and is well worth looking through, both for its beauty and for inspiration. It's possible to buy how-to books and kits that teach the basics of illumination and calligraphy. If you're lucky enough to live near a group from the Society of Creative Anachronism, you may find a teacher there.

Would you like to experiment with different alphabets or fonts? An Internet search can get you started with Egyptian hieroglyphs or with the Futhark, Ogham, Tengwar, or Theban alphabets, to name a few. These alphabets are usually handwritten, but it's possible to find them as computer fonts, too. And speaking of fonts, they can also be handwritten: go to your favorite Web browser and search for "handwritten fonts." Grab your pencil and get started!

The Best Practices

These guidelines will help you maximize your journaling experience:

- Write as often as you can—every day is ideal.

- Find the optimal time and place for journaling. Journaling often fails when it's put off until day's end when one is exhausted. Find the best time of day for the process, writing when you're alert and vibrant.

- Do you want to be a better writer? Read more books! Books contain 50 percent more "rare" words than does television.

- Stir it up: every now and then, journal differently, using a new time or place, different materials, or a fresh technique.

- Go back and review past entries regularly; the solstices and equinoxes are good times to do this. We can learn a lot by reflecting on past entries—this is one of the most valuable aspects of the process.

- Make it fun! Journaling should be something you look forward to.

Recommended Reading

Ballenger, Bruce. "The Importance of Writing Badly." Earbirding. 2001. http://earbirding.com/students/Ballenger-ImportanceOfWriting Badly.pdf.

The Book of Kells. Trinity College Dublin. www.tcd.ie/Library/bookofkells.

Didion, Joan. "On Keeping a Notebook." 1968. This essay is easy to find on the Web.

Lo, Lawrence. Ancient Scripts. www.ancientscripts.com/index.html.

Pesznecker, Susan. *Crafting Magick with Pen and Ink.* St. Paul, MN: Llewellyn, 2009.

Starr, Benjamin. "How Does the Act of Writing Affect Your Brain?" Visual News. May 28, 2013. www.visualnews.com/2013/05/28 /how-does-the-act-of-writing-affect-your-brain.

Susan "Moonwriter" Pesznecker *is a writer, college English teacher, nurse, and hearth Pagan/Druid living in northwestern Oregon. Sue holds a master's degree in professional writing and loves to read, watch the stars, camp with her wonder poodle, and work in her own biodynamic garden. She is co-founder of the Druid Grove of Two Coasts and the online Ars Viarum Magicarum: A Magical Conservatory (www.magicalconservatory.com). Sue has authored* The Magickal Retreat *(Llewellyn, 2012) and* Crafting Magick with Pen and Ink *(Llewellyn, 2009) and is a regular contributor to many of the Llewellyn annuals. Visit her at www.susanpesznecker.com and www.facebook.com/SusanMoonwriterPesznecker.*

Illustrator: Christa Marquez

Spiritual Cleansing at the Crossroads

Najah Lightfoot

Dawn breaks and the pale blue light of a new day illuminates the sky. I'm standing in the crossroads with my back to the eastern sky. I'm ready to throw my bathwater over my shoulder, prepared to release what no longer serves me. I'm ready to embrace a new beginning.

Tingles of energy rise from my feet to my arms, to my hands. Power surges through me as I speak my words of power and release. A shift has taken place. I am cleansed and renewed.

A cleansing at the crossroads can be just what we need to clear the air and

step onto a new path. I encourage you to step into the crossroads and heal thyself!

As Witches and practitioners, we perform many works for others, from saying prayers to holding public rituals and everything in between. And while we may be great at taking care of others, taking care of ourselves often seems to fall to the bottom of the list, leaving our empathetic and intuitive senses muddled and unclear. A cleansing at the crossroads can be just what we need to clear the spiritual air and step onto a new path.

Why the Crossroads?

Because the crossroads is a place of power. It is a portal, a vortex, a place of energy long held sacred by humanity. As Pagans, we know it is the powerful goddess Hecate who presides over the crossroads. In ancient times people left offerings to her, to ensure safe passage to all who ventured through her domain.

In Hoodoo, there is the "black man" at the crossroads. It is said that if you go to the crossroads at midnight and ask for help learning an art or a craft, the black man of the crossroads will answer your request.

Going to the crossroads at midnight is a rite that requires courage and preparation. It is a rite one must not enter into lightly. I've been to the crossroads at midnight, and it was a thrilling and life-changing experience. I didn't meet the black man, but I did receive answers to my prayers. One must be prepared to accept whatever shows up.

Not all crossroads need to be the T-square type. You can also use the crossroads of a railroad track. Have you ever noticed, when looking at a railroad sign, that the bottom half actually says "crossroad"? If you're a train lover like me and need the energy of moving in a new direction, standing at a railroad crossing while performing your rite can be an exhilarating experience!

Timing Your Rite

The cleansing rite of the crossroads is best performed during a waning moon. However, you don't need to wait for the moon to be in a certain phase to perform a spell.

For example, if your work is centered around prosperity and the moon is in its waxing phase, you might say, "I call abundance to me in all areas of my life," instead of using words of release that would be appropriate during a waning moon. This way, you are still using the power of the moon to enhance your spellwork, while being aware of its cycle.

If you are a savvy Witch who pays attention to clock hours, days of the week, and astrological cycles, you could get very specific about when you perform the rite.

For instance, you might time your cleansing rite to correspond to when the hour is falling from the top of the hour to the half hour. If you can imagine the hands on a clock, when the minute hand is falling, that would be the time for releasing work. When the minute hand is rising, that would be the time for increasing work.

If you are sensitive to Mercury retrogrades, you may choose to wait until Mercury goes direct to ensure your communications are clear.

You could choose to perform the work on a Friday, the day of the week that is named for the goddess Freya. Friday is a good day for love work and would be a good day for cleansing, if you are seeking to cleanse bad relationship juju from your life.

You could choose to do all or none of these things. However, the more thought and practice you put into the rite, the more powerful it will be.

Cleansing Rite at the Crossroads

The description I gave at the beginning of this article was from a cleansing rite I performed the morning of my birthday. What better time could there be to cleanse oneself of all the muck from the previous year than the morning of one's birthday! In addition, on that particular birthday, it was also a new moon, so I felt especially giddy about the prospect of beginning anew.

To perform the rite of cleansing at the crossroads, you will need to gather several things and have them ready the *night before* your rite. Believe me, you don't want to be running around at daybreak trying to get all your stuff together.

To perform this cleansing rite, you will need the following items:

- Cleansing herbs, such as rosemary, eucalyptus, or hyssop

- Olive oil or a condition oil of your choice

- Two tealight candles

- Clean clothes

- A basin to catch your infused water if you are using a shower

- A container to carry your bathwater to the crossroads

- Enough time in the morning to ensure you step into the crossroads as dawn is breaking

Morning of the Rite—Preparations

Rise without speaking to anyone. You are concentrating power within yourself, and you don't want to break the spell by speaking.

Bring two cups of water to a boil. Add the herbs to the water, cover the pot, and let steep for approximately ten minutes. The longer it steeps, the stronger it will become.

While the infusion is steeping, anoint your tealight candles with olive oil or with the condition oil you have chosen. A "condition oil" is an oil made to work upon specific spiritual conditions. There are several varieties and types. If you are not comfortable with or proficient in using condition oils, olive oil will work just fine.

Once you have anointed your tealights, place them outside your bath or shower so that you will step between them when you exit your bath.

By now, your infusion should be ready. Be sure to strain the herbs from the liquid. Dispose of the herbs by returning them to the earth. You could sprinkle them in your garden or even put them in your flowerpots. If you have neither of those, simply blow the herbs to the wind, with love. Carry your infused water to the bathroom.

Place your clean clothes next to your bath, so you can put them on once you are dry.

WASHING YOURSELF DOWN

If you're using a tub, be sure to plug it. If you're using a shower, place a basin large enough for you to stand in, in the bottom of the shower.

In the shower or bath, set down your container of infused water. In the shower or bath, set down the container you will use to carry your bathwater to the crossroads.

Light the tealights. Step into the shower or bath.

Call into your mind that which you seek to release. If you have prayers of release that are helpful to you, now is a good time to say them.

Call upon your Goddess or Gods to help you release that which no longer serves you. As your recite your prayers, pour the infused water over your head, allowing it to run down and over your body. Feel your troubles being washed away. Once you have poured the water over yourself, brush yourself downward with your hands.

Gather some of the bath-water into your container, and drain the remaining water from your bath. Take the container of water with you as you step from the bath, walking between the two tealights.

Allow yourself to air-dry, then put on your clean clothes.

GOING TO THE CROSSROADS

As an urban Witch, I use the crossroads in my neighborhood where the streets meet and form a T. If you live in the country, there may be several crossroads that meet your needs. Either way, finding a crossroads shouldn't be too difficult a task.

Once you know which crossroads you are going to use, prepare yourself to either drive or walk to the crossroads if possible.

You need not be concerned about being seen. As you have thoroughly prepared yourself for this rite, Spirit will be with you and you will pass by unnoticed. In addition, there usually aren't many people up at this hour of the day.

When you enter the crossroads with your bathwater, stand with your back to the east. Gather your intention and power, speak your words of release, and cast your bathwater over your left shoulder.

This next step is very important: *Do not look back over your shoulder.* You will be tempted, but don't do it. Not looking over your shoulder is an act of faith. You must have faith that your prayers have been heard. Looking back over your shoulder negates all the work you have done. Lastly, go home by a different route than the one by which you came. You have set upon a new route in life. There is no need to backtrack over the same way in which you arrived.

As you walk or drive back home, embrace the new beginning you have created for yourself. You have just performed a powerful rite. Feel its power, go forth, and carry on. Blessed be!

Najah Lightfoot *is a Priestess of the Goddess. She keeps her faith strong by following the Pagan Wheel of the Year. She is dedicated to keeping the Old Ways while living in these modern times. She is a certified Lucky Mojo Practitioner and has a passion for writing, ritual, magick, and movies. Najah keeps herself fit and healthy through the practice of Shao-lin Kung Fu. She can be found online at www.craftandconjure.com, www.facebook.com /priestessnajah, and twitter.com/Priestess_Najah.*

Illustrator: Kathleen Edwards

Adding Mindfulness to Our Lives

Barbara Ardinger

L et's be honest: sometimes we get so caught up in our covens and circles, in magic and affirmations and our tutelary gods and goddesses, that we forget where we live. But we are human beings who live in specific locations on the planet Earth. Are we aware of what our home actually looks like? More important, do we live right here in our bodies? Or are we floating in our heads in some other magical world? What's going on *right here*?

Many of us are familiar with mindfulness meditation. When we want to calm ourselves and relieve some of the stress the twenty-first century dumps on us, we sit in an erect posture that enhances the flow of our chi. Then we close our eyes, follow our breathing in and out and around, and (eventually) learn the truth of who we are.

Some practitioners of mindfulness meditation recommend keeping the eyes open and adopting a soft focus somewhere around our solar plexus chakra. Others use dance as a form of meditation. Some of us engage in a mindful walking meditation in which we experience the sensations that happen in our body as we move. We start with our breath, then pay attention to how our feet, legs, and hips feel as we walk. If you haven't tried this walking meditation, go outside and walk. You have to keep your eyes open, of course, so you don't walk into traffic or trees.

Those methods are all good, but as Woody Allen said, "Eighty percent of success is showing up." *Let's be present in our lives.* Let's show up, open our eyes, and pay attention to what's going on. And let's be grateful for our blessings and pay them forward.

Let's be present in our lives. Let's show up, open our eyes, and pay attention to what's going on. And let's be grateful for our blessings and pay them forward.

Here are some exercises that will help you pay more attention to your life.

Be Present

Take a daily break from your devices. Turn off your smartphone and put it out of the way. Hide your tablet. Close your laptop. Turn off your PC. Turn off the TV. Read a book that has real pages that you can really turn. And take a break from spellwork and your magical and metaphysical webinars, too. Taking a technology break for a little while every day can improve your health.

Where are you *right now*? How is your body arranged? Are you sitting? Standing? Lying down? Take several deep, easy breaths and get centered in your body. Get grounded. Be here now. (Ram Dass's advice is still good.)

Keep Your Eyes Open

If you're indoors, do an inventory of your furniture. Look at every piece, from your bed, to the chair you sit in when you eat breakfast, to your bookshelves. Go sunwise around each room and answer these questions: Where did this piece of furniture come from? Your parents' house? Did you buy it? At a yard sale? A furniture store? Was it given to you? By whom? How long have you had it? Have you repainted or decorated it? While you're at it, give your furniture some attention. Dusting and polishing are good.

Walk out the door of your home and look around. Count the trees you see. Can you name the birds that inhabit your neighborhood? If not, ask someone who knows (a good way to make a new friend). What other critters live nearby? Opossums, raccoons, squirrels, feral cats? Say hello to them. Look at the nearest garden, which may be your own or may be in pots on a porch or balcony. Say hello to the plants. You don't need devices to do any of these things, and they're all better for your eyesight than staring at a screen. A bonus: you don't need to multitask while pulling weeds in a garden or greeting crows and squirrels.

Pay Attention

How are you feeling *right this minute*? We all live in the physical bodies we were born into in this life. Stand up and stretch. Do a few bends and twists. How limber are you? Does any part of your body ache or hurt? Do an inventory. Before you start thinking that this

bruise or that sore muscle is merely the sign of a karmic task you assigned yourself between lives, consider how any injury or illness you may have affects your life. What to do? Go to a doctor! Whether you prefer a traditional allopathic physician or a holistic practitioner, go to see someone who can help you feel better. Show up and pay attention at the doctor's office. Take better care of your body. We do more effective magic when we're physically healthy.

When you go to work tomorrow (if you work outside your home), pay attention to both what you do every day and where you do it. First, consider your work. Is it satisfying to you? Are you a careful worker? Do you pay attention to details? Being employed is good, but would you rather be doing something else? How would you go about taking that step? Second, consider the space you occupy at work. Do you share it with anyone? How is the space divided up? Is that satisfactory? Does your part of the space—your workstation or office—need to be tidied up? Housecleaning is often a good way to start the day.

Pay attention when you drive, especially when yours isn't the only car on the street. Put both your phone and your Bluetooth out of reach in the back seat, and don't ever try to meditate as you drive. Keep your beta brain waves lively by being present and paying attention. Watch in all directions for cars and trucks and people on bicycles and motorcycles. Be aware of your speed. Yes, all this may sound obvious, but the U.S. Government Website for Distracted Driving tells us that 10 percent of people under age twenty involved in fatal crashes were distracted and that "engaging in visual-manual subtasks (such as reaching for a phone, dialing and texting) associated with the use of hand-held phones and other portable devices increased the risk of getting into a crash by three times" (www.distraction.gov/content/get-the-facts/facts-and-statistics.html).

Be Grateful

No matter the size of the space you live in, you live indoors. You have a home. You own handy things. You get enough to eat every day. You probably have furry friends who live with you and purr or wag their tails when they see you. You (presumably) have your health and your mental faculties. You have friends and you're part of a community, probably several communities, from circles that meet every full moon to cyber communities and friends on social media.

These are things to be grateful for. I'm sure you can think of more. Here's a tip I got from a friend who sponsors people at addiction meetings. Every night before you go to sleep, make a list of the many elements of your life for which you give thanks. Before you turn off the light, write them down and read the list aloud. Ponder them as you go to sleep.

Pay It Forward

The Goddess has given us more than we can imagine! We live in physical bodies on a beautiful blue and green planet. We can spread our attention and our gratitude around. We can work at our Muggle jobs and still do magic. We can be kind and polite to other people and care about and for our neighborhood. We must remember that local is global. That's why it's important to be fully present in our lives. When we show up and pay attention, we're blessing ourselves and the consciousness of the planet.

Barbara Ardinger, PhD (*www.barbaraardinger.com*) *is the author of* Secret Lives, *a novel about crones and other magical folks, and* Pagan Every Day, *a unique daybook of daily meditations. Her other books include* Goddess Meditations (*the first-ever book of meditations focusing on goddesses*), Finding New Goddesses (*a parody of goddess encyclopedias*), *and an earlier novel,* Quicksilver Moon (*which is realistic...except for the vampire*). *Her monthly blogs appear on her website and on* Feminism and Religion (*http://feminismandreligion.com*), *where she is a regular Pagan contributor. Her work has also been published in devotionals to Isis, Athena, and Brigid. Barbara lives in Long Beach, California, with her two rescued Maine coon cats, Schroedinger and Heisenberg.*

Illustrator: Jennifer Hewitson

Spice Up Your Magic

Ember Grant

Among the tools of the modern Witch are a variety of plant materials we use in our everyday lives, both magical and mundane. Dried herbs, leaves, roots, nuts, ground woods, and resins all have their place in the cupboard of the modern Witch. As I considered the use of herbs and spices in my magical practice, I realized that my uses tend to focus more on herbs than spices. I reach for the leafy plants I grow in my garden—the lavender, sage, rosemary, and so on—but rarely venture into the realm of spices, except when cooking.

When you think of spices, what comes to mind? For me, the word spice immediately conjures up the aroma of cinnamon, followed by other exotic scents, usually in the form of incense or the spices I use in cooking. But throughout the ages, spices have been used for more than just flavoring. They have been  used to summon gods and ward off demons, protect against illness, and arouse desire.

Interestingly, it was this aspect of arousal that actually caused spices to be seen as dangerous. Some of these foods were even forbidden in various times and places. The main reason for this objection was because these attributes were thought to encourage sinful behavior—gluttony, pride, and lust. Spices were mysterious and therefore sought after, expensive, and a symbol of indulgence in some cases. Exotic and seemingly rare, spices inspired voyages and monopolies. Located in mystical paradises and surrounded by fable and fantasy, their value skyrocketed. And many spices have been used as currency at various times in history.

In spiritual lore in the Middle Ages, "God, Christ, the Virgin and saints, the holy and royal dead commonly smelled of spices" (Turner). These are not original notions; Pagans thousands of years before that time told of gods and goddesses who possessed an unearthly aroma. And spices have been burned as incense since ancient times. The Romans often perfumed their bodies for rituals and to enhance the performance of athletes.

Spices were, of course, practical. They enhanced the flavor of food. Some slowed or killed bacteria. Egyptians used spices in their mummification process. And yes, many spices were used as aphrodisiacs. In fact, spices were actually condemned by some who felt they were an unnecessary indulgence, a mark of the foreign and mysterious. Calvinists were known to have preached against the sensual mystique of spices, believing that bland food was the path to salvation.

Today, it's hard to imagine such commotion over a tiny jar of spice that can be found in any supermarket for a few dollars. Yet spices do still hold allure for us. The smell of sweet bread or cake with cinnamon and nutmeg is something that most people associate with pleasant memories.

So what magic can we do with spices, other than cook with them?

It can be difficult to define a spice precisely, since people think about plants in different ways. Typically, spice refers to dried seeds, roots, or other parts of plants, rather than the leafy parts we associate with herbs. There are plants that some people call spices but others call herbs, and some classify them as both. Some spices are, in fact, dried flower buds or even berries. Some people would classify chili peppers as spices because they can be dried and ground. So the definition of a spice is flexible.

Modern Witches know there are many ways to approach the use of spices in magic. We can use essential oils of these plants, plants that have been dried and ground in loose form or incense, or the plant parts in raw form. Since essential oils can be costly and sometimes irritate the skin, and incense can be difficult to obtain with the exact spices needed (unless you make your own), we'll focus here on ground loose spices. The ones I've chosen to explore are inexpensive and easy to obtain, and most of us already have them in our kitchens. They're among the most common culinary spices and have value as herbal and cosmetic remedies as well as a rich history and folklore. Also, these spices are often combined with each other—especially cinnamon, cloves, ginger, and nutmeg. I'll bet you can already think of cakes, cookies, and breads you make that contain combinations or maybe all of these.

The Fab Five Magical Spices

I will investigate five prominent spices: cinnamon, cloves, ginger, nutmeg, and black pepper. Sure, there are others I could have included, but five seems like an ideal number.

Cinnamon

Associations: Sun, fire

Botanical Name: *Cinnamomum zeylanicum*

Magical Properties: Spirituality, prosperity, success, love, lust, passion.

These are tall, bushy evergreen trees of the laurel family. The tree develops yellowish-white flowers that turn into bluish-purple berries. The spice comes from the dried inner bark of the tree, which actually evolved to protect the plant from insects. This bark rolls up as it dries, creating the familiar cinnamon "sticks." True cinnamon comes from Sri Lanka; actually, much of our cinnamon is really cassia (*Cinnamomum cassia*, a tree related to true cinnamon) or a blend of cinnamon and cassia. At one time, cinnamon was worth more than its weight in gold.

Cinnamon is often used as a remedy for colds and upset stomach and even to freshen the breath. It was often associated with love, and numerous Greek gods and goddesses were described using this aroma. Cinnamon was burned to honor the sun and was often burned in temples for purification.

Cloves

Associations: Jupiter, fire

Botanical Names: *Syzygium aromaticum* (also *Eugenia caryophyllus, Caryophyllus aromaticus*)

Magical Properties: Protection, prosperity, dispel negativity, increase physical attraction (especially when mixed with cinnamon), happiness, nurturing.

The name is derived from the Latin word *clavus*, which means "nail." If you look at whole cloves, you can see why they earned this name. These are the dried flower buds of an evergreen tree that can reach a height of fifty feet. The flowers are bright red when mature.

Cloves are one of the earliest of medicinal plants. As with cinnamon, Sri Lanka is one of the sources. This spice is also good for digestion and to relieve an upset stomach.

Ginger

Associations: Mars, fire

Botanical Name: *Zingiber officinale*

Magical Properties: Magical potency, prosperity, love, passion.

We use the root, or rhizome, of ginger. Young plants yield fresh ginger; dried ginger often comes from older plants, which are more pungent. Ginger is native to tropical Asia. It's a perennial plant that can reach three feet in height and has long spikes of white or yellow flowers with streaks of purple.

Ginger tea has long been used to aid digestion and ease nausea; candied ginger is widely available and is often more palatable, since it's dusted with sugar.

Nutmeg

Associations: Mars, Jupiter, fire

Botanical Name: *Myristica fragrans*

Magical Properties: Good fortune, health, fidelity, happy home.

Nutmeg, most often sold in its ground form, is actually a seed. These seeds were once so prized that people would actually carve them from wood to deceive buyers. They're very hard, so they must be grated. These trees are difficult to grow and are found only in tropical climates. Interestingly, this tree produces the spice *mace* as well— mace is the red webbing that encases the seed. Nutmeg is found mainly in Indonesia.

Nutmeg is another digestive aid and is also said to help relieve headaches. Don't overeat it; it can be dangerous in large doses.

Black Pepper

Associations: Mars, fire

Botanical Name: *Piper nigrum*

Magical Properties: Protection, dispel negativity, enhance focus, increase strength and courage.

Native to South Asia, and not to be confused with pepper plants like bell or chili, this plant is a woody, climbing vine. The berries are picked and dried—different colors of pepper (red, black, white, green) depend on how they're processed. This was once the most expensive and most widely traded of all spices. Vietnam is the largest exporter of pepper.

And yes, you guessed it: this one is another digestive stimulant. See a pattern here? It is also used to relieve congestion.

You'll notice that all of these spices are associated with the element of fire—perfect for "spicing up" your magic. This is no coincidence. Spices are often considered "hot," so their association with the element of fire is appropriate.

Spices and Stones for Spells

Here are some combinations of spices and stones that are associated with the element of fire. Make a convenient and fragrant bundle of spices and stones using a tea bag or cloth with a tight weave, so the ground spices won't leak out. Or combine the ingredients in a small bowl or other container if you don't plan to carry it with you.

Attraction: Amber, cinnamon, and clove

Prosperity: Citrine, tiger eye, nutmeg, and cinnamon

Passion: Carnelian, ginger, and cinnamon

Good Fortune: Topaz, nutmeg, and clove

Protection: Pyrite, black pepper, and clove

Love Potion #5

This "potion" combines all five spices discussed here for love and attraction, along with qualities of courage, protection, and good fortune. It's the perfect blend for igniting passion in yourself or to use with a partner to rekindle a faltering flame. Plus, you can drink it, though don't overdo it. Just take a few sips or add it to another cup of tea.

Since the properties of these five spices are varied, you don't have to use this potion only for love and desire. You can rewrite the spell and charge it for other uses as needed. The numerology of the number five includes life, love, health, vitality, and sensory experiences; five is also associated with the goddess Venus.

You can make this infusion as strong or weak as you like, depending on how much water you use. Obviously, you should avoid drinking it if you are sensitive to any of these spices or are pregnant or nursing. If you do plan to drink it, consider adding a bit of honey. It tastes better if you drink it warm, plus the warmth adds to the stimulating effect. Otherwise, you can add it to a bath or use it to anoint candles and crystals.

This is a stimulating tonic. Remember, each of these spices is associated with the element of fire and has a slightly masculine association.

Empty out a tea bag (or buy empty ones to fill). The bag should have a tight weave to hold the finely ground spices. Mix five whole cloves, ten whole peppercorns, and a dash each of cinnamon, nutmeg, and ginger. Seal the tea bag—if you're reusing one, you may need to staple it closed—and steep in boiling water for a few minutes. The longer you steep it, the stronger the infusion will be. Cool the tonic as desired.

Visualize your goal or specific need. Remember, avoid attempting to force someone else's feelings or actions. This potion is ideal for use in an existing relationship to increase passion and fidelity while ensuring a protective and nurturing environment. You can also use it to give yourself a boost of courage, perhaps to take the first step in meeting someone or initiating a new relationship. Your specific goal is important to keep in mind.

Here's a chant to use (in iambic pentameter, of course):

Spices five in number mix and blend,
Love and passion spark as I intend.

Store any unused portion in a glass jar; it's best if used within a week. If you plan to drink it later, refrigerate it.

Other Uses for Spices

Additional uses of spices in magic include sprinkling them around candles or throwing a pinch of spice into a fire. You can also burn candles on a bed of spices either on a plate or in a cauldron or other container. Magical cooking with spices is a wonderful way to celebrate a sabbat or an esbat. The food and beverage preparation can be part of the ritual as well as the feast. And don't forget aromatherapy: inhale the scent of the spices while visualizing your goal and stating your intent.

Next time you're looking for a magical herb for a spell, consider adding the seductive scent of spice. Imagine how prized these plants used to be, and give them an honored place in your magical practice.

BIBLIOGRAPHY

A *Wiccan Formulary and Herbal* by A. J. Drew

Cinnamon by Lou Seibert Pappas

Cunningham's Encyclopedia of Magical Herbs by Scott Cunningham

The Herb and Spice Companion by Marcus A. Webb and Richard Craze

Magical Aromatherapy by Scott Cunningham

The Master Book of Herbalism by Paul Beyerl

Spice: The History of a Temptation by Jack Turner

Ember Grant *has been writing for the Llewellyn annuals since 2003. She is the author of two books,* Magical Candle Crafting *and* The Book of Crystal Spells. *Ember lives in Missouri and enjoys hiking, photography, and indulging in a variety of creative crafts. Visit her at embergrant.com.*

Illustrator: Tim Foley

The Magical and Spiritual Uses of Diet

Autumn Damiana

How people eat is a concept that defines a culture as completely as language does. Because all human beings have to eat, many customs, traditions, and practices have evolved around food and the consumption of it. These traditions may be simple or complex, easily identified food patterns or complicated, culturally defined dietary laws. Food *is* culture, and the sharing of food can be a powerful way to affirm bonds of race, ethnicity, religion, heritage, origin, tradition, and custom. Because Witches, Wiccans, Pagans, and other followers of Earth-centered religions are also a culture, we too have loosely defined food traditions and food customs, such as the "cakes and ale" segment of a Wiccan ritual. However, "diet" (as in "a way of eating") is not usually talked about, and perhaps should be explored as a spiritual component.

An Overview of Diet Types

There are literally hundreds of different diets. There also seem to be almost as many different ways to classify them! For simplicity's sake, I have taken what seem to be the most popular eating patterns and philosophies and sorted them into my own categories.

Vegetarian/Vegan Diets

There is a lot of confusion about the difference between vegetarian and vegan and the various subtypes. To simplify, vegetarians eat no meat, but they might eat eggs and/or dairy, whereas vegans will eat no animal protein whatsoever and may even avoid animal- or insect-derived products, such as honey, leather, silk, and cosmetic additives. This is why veganism is usually cited as a lifestyle instead of a diet, although dietary-only vegans exist. (I know one who manages her Crohn's disease through a vegan diet.) Pescetarians are vegetarians who will eat fish but no other meat. Fruitarians are vegans who eat only fruit, berries, seeds, and sometimes lettuces. And people who follow a raw food diet are usually vegetarian or vegan.

Restriction Diets

These are all diets low in or completely lacking one key component: low-sugar, sugar-free, no-salt, gluten-free, nut-free, etc. Low-calorie diets would also fit in this category. Although these types of diets are often used for weight loss, there are also medical applications: allergies to gluten or nuts, minimal salt intake to lower blood pressure,

reduced sugar/gluten diets for diabetes or for controlling ADHD or autism spectrum disorders, etc. Low-carb (carbohydrate) diets such as Atkins, the Zone, South Beach, and glycemic index diets are also used for weight loss, although the goal of these diets is to regulate insulin levels.

HERITAGE/RELIGIOUS DIETS

Most of these diets have ancient roots based on either religion or the heritage of a specific people, or sometimes both. The Islamic halal and the Jewish kashrut (kosher) diets are based on religious law and include instructions on what to eat, what to avoid, and how food should be prepared. However, some people who identify with these cultures follow the dietary guidelines even if they do not follow the religion. Heritage diets like the Mediterranean diet, Sonoma diet, African heritage diet, etc., emphasize a particular region or people, but can be followed by just about anyone who is so inclined.

Ancestral Diets

This group includes the Paleo (Paleolithic), Hunter/Gatherer, Caveman, and Stone Age diets, which are all very similar. They consist of eating what modern science believes that our ancient ancestors ate for thousands of years before we became agricultural civilizations: lots of meat, with greens, seeds, nuts, fruits, vegetables, and tubers—essentially what ancient people could hunt or gather. Benefits include having more energy, naturally getting fuller faster, and processing calories more efficiently.

Natural/Organic Diets

These are not really specific diet plans, but rather a lifestyle. There are no firm restrictions, except that eating should be defined by natural and organic standards, such as sustainability, biodiversity, and "locavorism," which is eating foods that are locally sourced and in season. Some followers of this diet feel that anything carrying the organic label is permissible. "Organic" loosely means food free of genetically modified organisms (GMOs), antibiotics, growth hormones, preservatives, chemical pesticides, chemical additives, etc. "Natural" is an even more ambiguous term, but usually refers to food that is processed as little as possible.

Fasting/Cleanse Diets

Restricting food intake or eliminating food altogether for various reasons (religion, culture, health, etc.) has been a common practice around the world for centuries. Also, our early ancestors could not always count on being able to find food, so the human body has developed the ability to fast for up to a few days without any lasting ill effects. Weight loss, renewed energy, and detoxification have been reported by many who have fasted or done a semi-fast or cleanse. In both fasting and cleansing, hydrating is crucial. Water and fruit/vegetable juice or "cleanse shakes" may be consumed.

Spiritual Implications of Diet

Here are some of the most common aspects of witchy living that may be impacted by how and what you eat, with suggestions regarding the diets just described.

THE WICCAN REDE

The "harm none" passage in this poem describing Wiccan ethics and moral codes is often used to justify vegetarian and vegan lifestyles. The Rede also says to "fairly take and fairly give," which could be interpreted to mean that what we eat is not as important as the balance of give and take…a call to stewardship of the earth. However, there are no right or wrong answers here, so if you believe that eating meat is a violation of the Rede, than maybe vegetarianism/veganism is for you.

ENVIRONMENTALISM

Clearly the welfare of the earth is important to an Earth-centered religion! As such, a magical diet may be one that emphasizes a low carbon footprint, including biodiversity, sustainability, and conservation. Natural/organic diets fit the bill because of their eco-friendliness, as do vegetarian/vegan and low-protein diets, because they eliminate or restrict the consumption of meat, which is less environmentally friendly to farm than plants.

Connection to Nature

Again, natural/organic diets are a good choice, since "living green" will keep you connected to nature, especially if you eat locally and seasonally. An ancestral diet is another possibility, as you are relying directly on the earth to provide for you the same way that our hunter/gatherer predecessors did for most of human history. Or try a heritage diet, since these emphasize nutritious whole foods prepared simply.

Ritual/Magical Workings

Here is where restriction diets and fasting/cleansing come into play. Generally speaking, abstaining from meat, processed food (sugar and carbs), and heavy meals before ritual will aid a magical working immensely. Instead, eat some fruits and vegetables, or try fasting for a few hours beforehand. Salt, because it is grounding, should also be avoided when journeying or working on the astral plane, but take care, because a no-salt diet can leave you feeling scatterbrained and spacey. Fasting and cleanse diets are another great way to boost spirituality, but doing too much of either can also sap your strength.

Honoring a Chosen Path

Some people grow up with a particular heritage or religion, like Judaism, and choose to incorporate these traditions, including diet, into their Pagan practice. Others may discover later in life that heritage diets can help play a part in deepening their beliefs, like a Greek/Roman Reconstructionist who discovers the Mediterranean diet. I myself went through a period where I ate a mixed ancestral/low-carb diet to honor and connect with the primordial, pre-agricultural mother goddesses depicted in ancient art, such as the famous Venus of Willendorf statue.

Pros and Cons of Controversial Foods

Now let's discuss the pros and cons of some controversial foods.

SUGAR

This ingredient is the current stamp of unhealthy junk foods and should be avoided for the most part. Processed forms of sugar such as sucrose, high-fructose corn syrup, dextrose, and maltodextrin are found in foods alongside high levels of salt, fat, chemical additives, and other undesirables. However, remember that foods such as fruit, grains, and alcohol have naturally occurring sugars and also need to be eaten in moderation when on a low-sugar or low-calorie diet. This can be a real hassle at Pagan gatherings, since there's usually an abundance of all three of these foods. Cakes and ale are literally two of them, and I've never been to a ritual that didn't offer fruit to eat. Consuming large amounts of sugar, even the natural kinds, can amp you up on a sugar high and then cause you to crash, making you tired, grouchy, and unfocused, so plan your eating strategy and magical workings accordingly.

MEAT (INCLUDING FISH/POULTRY/EGGS)

Animal welfare is an important issue to consider, but what about plant welfare? Many Witches, including myself, believe that plants are sentient beings deserving of respect, and are frustrated by any hierarchical system that belittles plant life as being inferior to animal life. Strictly speaking from a biological point of view, no one life form is more or less important than any other—all life is a web of interdependence, and even so-called "higher" life forms (including humans) all die and eventually get eaten by worms, bugs, bacteria, and plants. Therefore, I do not believe it's fundamentally wrong to eat meat—it's all just part of the circle of life! But there are more responsible ways to eat meat than most people know. Animals raised for consumption do exhaust more resources than crops, are harder on the environment, and all too often are bred, kept, and/or slaughtered using cruel and inhumane methods. If you do eat meat, limiting your consumption as well as being aware of how to choose sustainably

and humanely raised meat will make this decision more ethical. Better yet, raise the animals yourself if you can!

"Wild" Foods

It may seem like a great idea to start hunting wild game or eat foraged wild plants, but there is a steep learning curve associated with these practices. For starters, do you know the hunting laws, seasons, locations, and licenses required in your area? How about how to find and track your prey, and the safe use of guns, bows, knives, etc.? Foraging comes with its own set of problems, too. Mushrooms and other edible look-alikes can kill you or put you in the hospital if you eat the wrong ones. And let's not forget: some species are off-limits because they are endangered or protected. So if you are interested in harvesting wild food, sign up for a beginner course in hunting or foraging and get the necessary information you need beforehand.

Alcohol (and Other Intoxicants)

The common consensus among Pagans is to be pretty permissive about the use of alcohol, but it is largely frowned upon in ritual, and most circles will restrict the consumption of it to after the working or ban its use altogether. Conversely, some Pagan groups, such as Druids and Norse/Germanic Heathens, have a reputation for mixing alcohol with religion on a regular basis! The same can be said of any intoxicant: some people use them to deliberately induce an altered state, and some believe that sobriety is key to successful focus and direction in ritual. Again, the cakes and ale ceremony, which often includes ale (beer), mead, wine, or other spirits, is fairly prevalent in witchy company. Both the Wiccan Rede and the Charge of the Goddess also mention wine. In any case, the use of intoxicants is ultimately up to each individual, coven, or group, but BEWARE of anyone, Pagan or otherwise, who forces you to get intoxicated for any reason, as this is a sure sign of danger!

Coffee/Chocolate/Tobacco

Most Pagans I know would throw a fit if either coffee or chocolate were taken away from them. But these two foods are not as harmless as they seem—both are stimulants, and those who believe that alcohol has no place in the circle because it artificially alters consciousness might also want to reconsider coffee and chocolate, which can contain high levels of sugar and/or caffeine. The same is true of tobacco, which, while not a food per se, is still used by Native Americans, shamans, Hoodoo practitioners, etc., for spiritual purposes, but is also a stimulant and is seriously addictive. Adding to the confusion, all three of these "commodities" are questionable in their sustainability. Every year worldwide, many thousands of acres of rainforest or land that could be used to cultivate food are used to grow these cash crops instead. The farmers and workers who grow these commodities are often exploited and underpaid. In addition, all three of these crops are subject to genetic engineering, heavy pesticide treatment, irradiation, and chemical processing.

Just as with meat, limit your consumption of coffee, chocolate, and tobacco. Do your research and find the ethical alternatives.

Feasting

The one eating pattern I have not yet addressed is feasting. Feasting goes hand in hand with holidays and is part of every food culture. While overindulgence is generally viewed as negative, it is usually permissible during a feast to overeat, drink too much, or consume otherwise prohibited specialties, because feasting serves another purpose. Feasting is about celebration, and may be a necessary purge before or after more ceremonial and restrictive events, like the Mardi Gras phenomenon that precedes Lent or the ancient Beltane festivals that heralded the end of the dark half of the year.

. . . .

I hope that I have awakened your interest in the magical uses of diet and that you will be more mindful of what you eat on your spiritual path. Just like any other aspect of life, your diet can be a useful tool to guide you or to enhance your magical journey. I hope this article will speak to you in such a way that it sparks a conversation, prompts you to do your own research, or changes the way you view the food you eat in relation to your magical lifestyle.

PRINT RESOURCES

Bonewits, Philip Emmons Isaac. *Neopagan Rites: A Guide to Creating Public Rituals That Work.* Woodbury, MN: Llewellyn Publications, 2007.

Cunningham, Scott. *Cunningham's Encyclopedia of Wicca in the Kitchen.* St. Paul, MN: Llewellyn Publications, 2003.

Pollan, Michael. *In Defense of Food: An Eater's Manifesto.* New York: Penguin, 2008.

Meat and Seafood Resources

http://certifiedhumane.org

www.compassionate-carnivores.org

www.humaneitarian.org

www.seafoodwatch.org

www.stopfactoryfarms.org

Wild Food Resources

www.ediblewildfood.com

www.ihea.com

www.wheretohunt.org

www.wildfoodadventures.com

Heritage Diets

http://oldwayspt.org

Autumn Damiana *is a writer, artist, crafter, and amateur photographer, and has been a mostly solitary eclectic Witch for fourteen years. She is passionate about eco-friendly living and writes about this and her day-to-day walk on the Pagan path in her blog "Sacred Survival in a Mundane World" at http://autumndamiana.blogspot.com. When she's not writing or making art, you can find her outside enjoying nature or investigating local history in her hometown of San Jose, California. Contact her at autumndamiana@ gmail.com.*

Illustrator: Kathleen Edwards

Witchcraft Essentials

Practices, Rituals & Spells

Magical Kids

Jane Meredith

Doing magic and spells with kids can be fun, simple, and effective. Unlike adults, children don't usually need convincing that magic is real, and for them, the shifts between imagination and reality are much more familiar. They are happy to work with allies—unseen, animal or plant, and toys—and bring their whole selves into magical workings, just as they would into a game, storytelling, or an adventure. In fact, magic that is a mix of a game, a story, and an adventure is perfect for them. Magic spells can also be a gentle way to approach difficult topics such as settling into a new school or dealing with nightmares or illness.

Here are three magic spells to work with children. I've written them for a child between the ages of four and ten, but adapt them as needed. There's a gingerbread spell to change reality, a spell to counter nightmares, and a healing spell. They work for adults as well! When working magic for or with someone, whether child or adult, it's important to let them do some or most of the work—to make the decisions and only take the next step when they're ready. You can set up a spell for someone else and guide them through it, but ultimately it has to be their spell if it's to work for them, even if the person is only three years old.

Gingerbread Spell to Change Reality

This spell is great when a hesitancy arises over some stage of growing up. I have used it for very concrete realities that can be measured, rather than emotional developments that might be harder to track.

Start with one gingerbread person. For added magical power, you could make your own, although I've used purchased ones successfully.

You'll need an altar or other special place to do this spell. You can spend some time with the child choosing the location of the altar and what will be on it, preparing them for the magic.

Introduce the gingerbread person to the altar, naming its special quality. For example: "This gingerbread person is able to go to sleep in a room by himself," "This gingerbread person takes the bus to school," "This gingerbread person makes her own breakfast," or whatever the desired ability is. Keep the spell as simple as possible, and use only one quality for the gingerbread person to hold. If you want, create some symbol to further emphasize the skill or nature of the gingerbread person. For the previous examples, you might give the gingerbread person a small blanket, a picture of a bus, or a spoon.

Leave the gingerbread person on the altar. There should be some anticipation involved—at least one day's worth, but maybe more. During this time, keep referring back to the gingerbread person and its quality. You can tell little stories about how the gingerbread person can do that special thing, maybe how it was the very first time the gingerbread person did that thing. Make it very clear that this ability is an essential part of the gingerbread person and anyone eating it will automatically have that quality transferred to them.

When the child is ready, let them eat the gingerbread person, ingesting its quality. Having made it very clear that eating the gingerbread person *will* result in the quality becoming the child's, let them know that they can't eat it unless they are willing for this to happen. Wait for the child to choose this; before they eat it, emphasize again that they must be ready to take on this quality.

Have fun and don't forget to thank the gingerbread person!

Bedtime Guardians:
A Spell to Deal with Nightmares

This spell is a way of giving a child more awareness and strategies to deal with nightmares and night fears. The purpose is not primarily to *prevent* nightmares, but rather to invite guardians to be present within the child's dreaming and waking. This spell can be set up over a number of consecutive nights and then reinforced regularly to build a continuing sense of safety and power. After a while, teach the child to reinforce it by themselves.

Figure out the compass directions of the child's bed; hopefully the corners of the bed are somewhat aligned with the four major directions. Do all of the work for this spell and all of its reinforcements with the child lying down in the bed, ready for sleep. Talk with the child about the elements and how each element has many guardians, beings, and animals that live within that element and are associated with it. For example, ask the child how many different types of guardians they can think of that live in the water.

Then, to set the spell, begin with the element of air in the east. Show the child which corner of the bed (or perhaps it is a side of the bed) corresponds with east, and describe many types of air to them, such as breezes, storms, and breath. Then ask them to imagine a special being, from the air, to come and live there, on their bedpost or in the air just above that corner of the bed, to guard them during this night and all nights. Accept the child's answer, whether it be fairy or bird or spirit or dragonfly. Work with the child to summon and imagine this guardian coming to take up residence at the east point.

If your child is young, setting one guardian a night will be enough. On the second night, after greeting and reconfirming the presence of the air guardian, proceed to fire (in the Southern Hemisphere, it will be north; in the Northern Hemisphere, it will be south), and do the same thing. Fire may be a more difficult element for which to think of a guardian, although there are dragons, salamanders, and phoenixes. Help the child with a variety of suggestions if they get stuck.

Continue nightly. With an older child, all four guardians can be chosen and set on one night. The water guardian will be in the west, and the child may choose a fish, whale, mermaid, or frog. The earth guardian will be in the north for the Northern Hemisphere and in the south for the Southern Hemisphere. For this element, the child may choose a wild or domestic animal, a tree, or a rock.

On subsequent nights, continue to mention and greet these guardians once the child is in bed and ready for sleep. In later discussions about dreams, or during the night if your child can't fall sleep, ask the child to choose the appropriate guardian to take with them back into sleep, or into a dream, or talk about how a particular guardian may be able to help them in a dream or a state of anxious wakefulness.

You can also do visualizations of the guardians or guided journeys with one or more of the guardians before sleep.

Healing Spell to Work with Kids

This healing spell alleviates the feelings of helplessness and fear that children can experience around illness, giving them both a chance to discuss it and a way to help. I found that my son, even at age five or six, could sense the difference between someone who was sick and someone who was dying, and would choose and send appropriate energies. When making the healing spell, he was also able to ask questions about death and make illness and dying a little less of an intimidating, adults-only realm. I've used this spell with children to work with someone else's illness, but it could also be used with an ill child to assist in their own healing.

Find a quiet time and place to do this spell. It might take only ten minutes or as long as thirty minutes, and it's good to plan a quiet "coming down" time after it, in case there are questions or feelings to discuss. It's best to do this spell in the morning, away from bedtime and when the child isn't tired.

This spell should remain child-centered. The adult should outline the idea and give suggestions but take cues from the child as to the depth and direction of the spell. Remember, the purpose of the spell is to allow the child to feel involved and empowered, so if it doesn't go the way you want or imagined, you might have to do your own spell separately.

Lay the groundwork by talking with the child about the person who is sick. You might want to have a photo or token of that person present, or take the time to explain the nature of the sickness and its likely progression. Let the child ask questions, and then sit together for a few moments, imagining how the sick person might feel. Then explain that you are going to use four elemental energies (or five, if you prefer) to make a circle and help the spell to work. For each energy, you'll need a helper; you could choose a soft toy or use magical things such as wands, candles, crystals, or natural items such as flowers or feathers. The crucial point is that the child is the one choosing them.

The first elemental energy is air. These are the thoughts the child wishes to send to the sick person. Talk with the child about what sort of thoughts they would be and then have the child choose a helper.

The helper should be something that will assist these types of thoughts. So if the child wishes to send comforting thoughts to the sick person, the helper should be comforting; if the child wishes to send happy thoughts, the helper should lend itself to happiness. Get the helper and place it in the circle with you.

If you wish and the child is familiar with directional magic, you can place this air helper in the east.

The second elemental energy is fire. This is the power or energy you are sending into the healing—gentle or strong, sudden or gradual. Once again, talk a little about this, drawing the child's ideas out. Then let the child find a helper to transmit the energy, and place the helper in the circle with you. The child may choose something obviously associated with fire or energy, such as a candle, or the link may be more abstract, such as a toy elephant for a strong healing. If you are working directionally, the fire helper will be placed in the south if you are in the Northern Hemisphere, or in the north if you are in the Southern Hemisphere.

The third elemental energy is water. This is about an emotional aspect of the healing, the feelings involved. The child might simply wish to send love. They might also, or instead, be working with accepting grief, loss, or fear. Once again, talk about it, being guided by the child as to the depth and length of the discussion. Then have the child find a helper to transmit that energy, and place the helper in the circle with you. If you are working directionally, this water helper will be in the west.

The fourth elemental energy is earth. This part of the healing spell is about comfort, safety, and being looked after. Talk with the child about what makes a person feel safe and comforted and how that might feel for the sick person. Have the child find a helper to transmit that energy, and place the helper in the circle with you. If you are working directionally, this earth helper will be in the north if you are in the Northern Hemisphere, and in the south for the Southern Hemisphere.

The fifth elemental energy is spirit (if you are using five elemental energies). I would only do this step with an older child who can hold the focus longer and has a clear relationship to spirit. Proceed as before, and if you are working directionally, place the helper in the center of your circle.

To anchor the spell, sit quietly or sing a little song together, focusing on sending your wishes to the helpers so that they can carry out this healing spell. You can leave the circle set up for a while or disperse it. Later, discuss the qualities of the spell (the thoughts, energy, and emotions of the spell) and how the child feels the healing spell went. The child may choose to check in with the helpers or later repeat the spell.

Jane Meredith *is an author and ritualist who lives in Australia. Her books include* Circle of Eight: Creating Magic for Your Place on Earth, Rituals of Celebration, *and* Journey to the Dark Goddess. *Jane is passionate about participative ritual, invocation of the divine, trees, rivers, and mythology. She offers workshops and distance courses. Visit her website at www.janemeredith.com.*

Illustrator: Jennifer Hewitson

From Shadows to Light: An Overview of Banishing and Polarization

Michael Furie

Standing in the center of the troubled house and working clockwise throughout the entire dwelling, the Witch feels his power grow with ever-increasing intensity as he casts pentagrams in the air at each window and door, forming an impenetrable force from which the entity cannot escape. The etheric creature, caught in the wave of this powerful energy field, is pushed outward and away, dislodged from its unwelcome occupation and expelled back to whence it came. Afterward, the Witch, knowing that the energy vacuum caused by the spirit's extrication must be resolved to avoid reinfestation, blesses the house in order to restore the energetic balance.

. . . .

By the flickering light of twin black candles, as the carefully blended incense drifts up from the cauldron, the Witch writes the the name of the harmful person or habit on a piece of paper and wills his energy into the paper with the intent that the negative subject of the spell be cast out of his life, that all ties be cut and peace return. The Witch then drops the paper into the cauldron, and as the smoldering incense flares and the paper ignites, the energy bursts forth and is released, instantly reaching the target of the spell and beginning to alter the patterns of probability, bending them toward the magical goal.

These are two examples of banishing. The word *banishing* is commonly defined as "to forbid, abolish, or get rid of, as in sending away something unwanted." Banishing magic can be a powerful recourse when nothing else seems to adequately address the problem, when no amount of reasoning, cleansing, or blessing seems to be able to end the situation. Generally speaking, when we use magic to banish an energetic some-*thing*, we are creating an energy field strong enough to push an opposing force away from us. It's sort of like getting a ball out of a bucket by filling the bucket with water until the ball spills out over the side. The ball is an opposing force in the bucket, taking up space that we would rather have filled by the water.

Banishing magic can be a powerful recourse when nothing else seems to adequately address the problem, when no amount of reasoning, cleansing, or blessing seems to be able to end the situation.

ter. The powerful water surrounds the ball, moves it, and banishes it from the bucket. This is a simplistic comparison, to be sure, but it's essentially accurate.

When a person or habit is banished, the energy operates a bit differently. When trying to banish a habit, we're affecting our own mind, using energy and affirmation to reprogram our subconscious so we have less desire to engage in the habitual behavior. It's important to recognize and utilize the magical (i.e., energetic) aspects of the working to maximize its effectiveness; otherwise we are just using positive thinking without creating lasting subconscious reinforcement. When we use magical power on ourselves, it acts as a continual transmission of our message and gradually steers us in the right direction.

This is also true when banishing a person from your life. The energy packet of intent is sent from the spell into the person's subconscious mind. From there, the power of the message is transmitted to the person, compelling them to leave us alone. This can be much more difficult to achieve

than working on ourselves, since people have a natural psychic defense against outside influences. Ethical considerations aside, such as tampering with someone's free will and the potential magical rebound, a strong reason for not using banishing spells on people is the enormous amount of work they can require. If a person is merely bothersome as opposed to outright harmful, it is usually not worth the time and effort it takes to magically banish them from our lives. If a person is causing genuine harm, however, their wrongful actions weaken their own psychic defenses and actually enable us to banish them much more easily. It's a magical paradox that when a person causes harm, it makes it easier for them to also be harmed. This is one way that the law of return ensures balance.

Another similar technique used by Witches to rid the environment of negativity is *polarization*. The concept of polarization is rooted in the Hermetic principles, seven universal laws regarding the nature of existence. These principles are believed to have originated in the teachings of Hermes Trismegistus, who was said to be a sage and/or a god (depending on interpretation) dating back to ancient Egypt. The Hermetic teachings are considered to be one of the pillars of Western esoteric philosophy and have been written about and taught in

alchemy, ceremonial magic, and some Witchcraft traditions. Their philosophical implications as well as their practical magical applications have been explored. The most popular resource on them is a book called *The Kybalion*, published anonymously by a person or group called "the Three Initiates."

I was taught that many of the greatest secrets of Witchcraft are found through the resolution of paradoxes. The truth of this statement was beyond my understanding until I learned about the Hermetic principle of polarity. This principle states that everything has a dual nature; all things have their opposites, and these opposites are identical in nature, differing only by degree. An example of this is temperature. Hot and cold are opposites, yet they are merely the underlying polarity of the overall concept of temperature. The degrees of what is termed hot and what is termed cold are largely subjective, though this doesn't invalidate their nature as opposites; it, in fact, illustrates the point that opposites are identical. Continuing with this example, polarizing the opposing forces would simply be a matter of reconciling hot with cold, such as combining cold water with hot water and ending up with their balance, the neutral tepid water.

It is the same with energy. Energy is constant, but since it carries an intentional charge, its poles, much like with magnetism, are categorized as positive and negative. Since energy is everywhere, we're all touched in some way by its level of polarization, its feel or vibe. When negativity is too strong in a specific location, such as a room in a house, there can be a level of discomfort that in some cases almost amounts to a haunting. In situations like this, there can be cold spots, noises, objects that move or go missing without explanation, or just a general feeling of fear or unease. This type of energy disturbance can be banished, but in order to banish, one must send energy away; and if this energy is still negatively charged, the location where it ends up can be filled with the same type of disturbance. In polarizing energy, we take the problem energy and transmute its negative vibration to the positive pole. We are left with positive energy and a restored calm in the room. Even if we choose to then banish the energy, it will be free of disturbance wherever it is sent.

A closely related practice to polarization used by many is *reiving*, which is the name used by some Witchcraft traditions for the pre-ritual cleansing of the circle (and for the cleansing of a space, in general). Practically speaking, reiving usually consists of one or more of the following: sweeping with the ritual broom (usually without the bristles actually touching the ground), sprinkling consecrated saltwater, and/or circulating a cleansing incense around the circle. Whatever methods are used, the purpose of reiving is to "rend asunder" the astral buildup in the atmosphere of the site, leaving the area spiritually clear and ready for ritual. Reiving amounts to an aggressive form of polarization; the negativity is agitated and stirred up out of its entrenchment and transformed through magical intent to be positive or at least neutral.

Regardless of form, polarization is an excellent means of restoring the proper balance and calm to the atmosphere of a place that has been subject to any type of mental, emotional, or spiritual turbulence, such as quarreling, illness, or extended depression. It's an effective technique when unwanted visitors have left but the uncomfortable residue of their disruptive energies still lingers and a return to a harmonious environment is needed.

> **Polarization is an excellent means of restoring the proper balance and calm to the atmosphere of a place that has been subject to any type of mental, emotional, or spiritual turbulence, such as quarreling, illness, or extended depression.**

A good, basic form of polarization requires no tools and can be done at any time. It is a combination of meditation and energy work that can quickly restore the balance to a room. The first step is to shift one's consciousness into a meditative state through a meditation, such as the Rainbow Meditation that was included in my book *Spellcasting for Beginners*. Here are the instructions.

Make yourself comfortable in the room needing polarization, and close your eyes. Breathe in and out gently and evenly, and see yourself outdoors, floating on a cloud. The cloud floats upward, sailing over the top of a rainbow. At this point, the cloud begins to descend into the rainbow, and you find yourself surrounded by color. You begin to feel the slow descent, and your field of vision is colored red.

All you see is red as you pass through this part of the rainbow. Slowly, you sink deeper into the rainbow, and now your vision changes and all you see is orange. The color glows and feels like being out in warm sunshine. As you drift farther down, you move into yellow, and everything is as fresh and bright as daffodils. Moving deeper into the rainbow, you now find yourself surrounded by crisp, spring green. As you continue, you move into beautiful sky blue, then dark, cool indigo. Your journey is almost complete as you finally sink into the violet sphere of spirituality. Once you are in violet, say to yourself, "I have traveled through the spectrum and have reached a spiritual level of power and comfort."

Once you have reached this point, visualize yourself back in the room and imagine you're holding an old-fashioned "scales of justice" type of scale. Mentally pull all the energy from the room, and see it swirling in a ball on the left side of the scale. Visualize it as a color you find unpleasant or that represents negativity. See this ball of energy as being so thick and heavy that it weighs down the left side of the scale. Place a ball of balanced energy on the right side of the scale in a color that you feel expresses calm and balance, the direct opposite of the imbalanced energy on the left. In your mind's eye, watch the scale come into equilibrium, and see each side glow with only the balanced energy. Finally, mentally release the energy back into the room, and see both sides of the scale as empty. Watch the scale vanish, then visualize yourself back at the rainbow. To end this meditation, imagine yourself being drawn up, back through the colors and out of the rainbow in reverse. Incidentally, I use left as the receiving side and right as the projecting side, as this is my traditional practice; some people may choose to reverse the directions.

Polarization can be used to neutralize the effects of bothersome individuals (or groups) in our lives without the same potential ethical or rebound issues associated with actual banishing, making it my

preferred choice for dealing with difficult (but not blatantly harmful) people. To do this, use the Rainbow Meditation, and once in violet level, visualize the problem person and see them sending negativity toward you, like dark smoke. Mentally encase the person and their energy in a bubble of white light, then see the dark smoke they are trying to send as bright light smoke or waves swirling back around them, thus keeping them from being able to cause trouble.

In the past, I haven't written very much about banishing for two reasons: it can be a tricky thing to accomplish without unpleasant consequences, and most of us really don't have the need to outright banish something or someone very often. Polarization and neutralizing harm are far more relevant in our lives. We can use these tools, which are also surprisingly sophisticated magical techniques, as often as desired without magical backlash.

Michael Furie (*Northern California*) *is the author of* Spellcasting for Beginners *and* Supermarket Magic, *both published by Llewellyn, and has been a practicing Witch for over twenty years. An American Witch, he practices in the Irish tradition and is a priest of the Cailleach. You can find him online at www.michaelfurie.com.*

Illustrator: Christa Marquez

Easy Guide to
Guided Meditations

Blake Octavian Blair

Witches and Pagans have long enjoyed and known the value of
meditation. Guided meditations often
have an extra layer of appeal, as they
can be designed for specific purposes or
goals and even group workings. While
many practitioners have their favorites
they turn to within the magickal vol-
umes on their bookshelves, they hesi-
tate or falter when they cannot find one
that perfectly suits their needs and/or
they must find where exactly to begin
the process of creating their own. The

good news is that it's not difficult to create your own guided meditations, and it can be a wonderful creative exercise!

Purposes of Guided Meditations

When broken down into steps, learning to create your own guided meditations is an easy and enjoyable process. The first step is to decide what the purpose of the guided meditation you are creating will be. Guided meditations have many purposes, so let's take a look at a few of the more common ones among magickal practitioners.

GROUNDING AND CENTERING

At the beginning of a group ritual, class, or workshop, or even a more businesses-style meeting of magickal-minded folk, it is always a good idea to make sure all participants are beginning the event from a grounded and centered place. A guided meditation is not only an easy way to accomplish this as a group with a shared visualization, but it also aids in melding the energies of all the individuals into a cohesive whole for the time they are together.

CREATING SACRED SPACE

Visualization is powerful. There is a famous quotation of the Buddha that states that with our thoughts, we create the world. Through meditation, we can manifest many goals, including the creation of sacred space.

PROTECTION

We all want to surround ourselves with protective energy, whether we are just beginning a work day, traveling a long distance, or starting a magickal working. The process of a guided meditation can help to raise, grow, and strengthen that energy.

Healing

A guided meditation can be used to work with healing energy for both yourself and others, near and far. A meditation can help put you in the proper mindset to engage in healing work from a calm place.

Encountering Spiritual Beings

Either as a goal in and of itself or as a preparation for work about to be undertaken, a guided meditation can be designed and utilized to encounter spiritual beings. Perhaps it is a particular archangel or protector, or even a manifestation of a part of yourself—for example, your "creative self" or the "divine feminine within yourself."

The themes, purposes, and focuses of potential guided meditations are endless. Feel free to get creative to meet your needs!

Creation Process

Now let's get down to the nitty gritty of creating a guided meditation. First you will need to decide if the meditation is to be experienced by a group or a single individual. Next, determine whether those experiencing the meditation will be working toward individual goals (such as meeting a manifestation of a part of themselves) or toward a common goal (such as grounding and centering for a group ritual that is to follow or to send distance healing to a particular place or event). Once you decide on those factors, you will know the path and direction the meditation must take.

A guided meditation usually is experienced by the participant as an act of observance. You observe what is happening and being described by the narrator. It is a more passive than active experience. This is not to say that you will not be told to take some action during the course of the meditation; however, the main goal will be to observe things as they come to you and unfold before you. A guided meditation can often be described as watching an ethereal movie in your mind.

In general, I feel that when creating a guided meditation, you want it to guide but not be too leading. What I mean by that is that I don't like to give the participants a lot of suggestive or exact details. I might say, "You will notice a beautiful temple appear upon the landscape." I have not described what the temple or the landscape looks like, so the person is left to freely interpret it in the way that is proper and correct for them. This helps to maintain the individual experience rather than one created for them. The participants are still guided in their process so that they can reach the goal or intention for which you have designed the meditation (as opposed to the more spontaneous, freeform, and active shamanic journey—which is a separate topic entirely). However, giving the participants autonomy in how the experience manifests further allows it to be a true spiritual experience rather than simply a narration of fanciful fiction (we're not learning about how to write books on tape!).

A partial exception to leaving the details of the visualization as wide open to the individual participants as possible is when there is a unified and very specific group goal for the meditation. An example would be sending healing to a specific location of an event. To unify the energy and intent, you might give a very specific description of the location on which you are setting your intention to receive the healing. For example, you might ask all the participants to visualize the area as being surrounded by a certain color of healing light.

In this case, you are tapping into the increased power of a number of individuals sending the same signal out into the ethers with a unified vision. The old saying "There is power in numbers" holds true metaphysically.

Creating a Framework for the Meditation

It is good to have in mind a general structure or framework around which to build your meditation. A general outline you may want to follow would include the following steps:

1. Physically setting the tone in the space.

2. Bringing the participants into a state of calm and relaxation, stating and setting the intention/goal, then guiding the participants to a destination, a place, or an entity.

3. Having an encounter to accomplish the intention/goal.

4. Guiding the participants out of the space and meditation.

5. Possibly a re-grounding.

A guided meditation is a ritual working and form of magick all on its own, in my opinion. Therefore, as with any other working, I feel it's a good idea to put some preparation into the meditation space. A good energetic cleansing through smudging with sage or another sacred herb, the asperging of holy water, the ringing of a singing bowl, or the shaking of a rattle all work quite well. Dimming the lights can also help to set the mood and create a soothing atmosphere. This step may seem simple and not take very long, but I feel it lays an important foundation.

Next you will want to lead the participants through a series of instructions and visualizations that will bring them into a calm and

relaxed state. One classic way to do this is to have them close their eyes and then have them start at their feet and focus on body parts one by one: feet, to ankles, to legs, to torso, and so on, working all the way to the head. Another classic method is to have them visualize themselves as a tree, with their legs as roots, growing down into the earth. I find both methods to be effective for relaxation and grounding simultaneously. An additional simple method is to have the participants count backward from a sacred or symbolically significant number (such as eleven, which is considered to balance masculine and feminine energies). With any method, a tip to remember is to focus on relaxed breathing—deep breaths in and cleansing exhalations out. Be creative with your descriptions of the methods and with developing your own new methods! Just prior to starting or after ending the verbally guided relaxation, some practitioners like to ring a meditation chime or soft bell or play a singing bowl to add to the energy, as an added touch.

Now comes the meat of the guided meditation proper. You need to decide on a general type of destination to which you would like to guide your participants, where they will experience the relevant action pertaining to the goal/intent. You also need a path to lead them there. I like to let the path appear to them however it is meant to appear for them within the context of the experience. It is around this point in time that I like to verbally set the intention of the meditation. For example, I may say: "Today we are going to meet the manifestation of our own creative spirit, however and in whatever form it wishes to appear to you. Take a deep, relaxing breath and see yourself surrounded by nature. The temperature is perfect and the weather is beautiful. You notice a path before you. You begin to follow it…" The destination can be one of an endless number of possible locations; however, common go-to options include open fields, natural bodies of water, temples, or even houses. Remember, when you guide the participants, your descriptions will ideally be left a bit vague so as to not control their experience too tightly, allowing them to visualize *their* temple, body of water, or field as it manifests in the correct and best way for them.

I have given the next phase or component the working title "the encounter." Once the participants have "arrived" at the destination, this is where the action revolving around the intent and meat of the experience is observed. They ask the entity they are encountering for a message. The entity gives them a symbolic gift for a purpose or message, or sometimes the participants simply observe and wait for a message to appear. For example, some lines from the meditation may read, "After observing the details of how your creative spirit appears to you, you notice it has a gift for you, to assist you with your creative endeavors. Think about what the gift means and how you are to utilize it." Alternatively, the participants could arrive at their destination and you could simply say, "Find a comfortable place in the natural landscape to sit and observe the horizon. Make note of any beings, animal or human, that may appear, and how they behave. Think about what message this might be conveying to you." Sometimes the encounter is not with another being but with oneself. Perhaps the participants visualize themselves turning into a tree or a certain type of crystal. Perhaps they observe themselves surrounded by a certain color of light for a particular purpose. Before this phase of the meditation ends, it is a good time to ensure that you guide the participants in any affirmations you wish to include before guiding them out of the meditative experience. Here is an example: "Say to yourself, 'I have a creative spirit. I am a creative being.'"

The next step is to guide the participants out of the encounter and away from the destination. This is relatively easy to accomplish. First, if the meditation guided them to encounter any entities, guide the participants to thank them for their messages. Then, tell the participants to exit the temple, leave the field, etc., and follow the path they came in on to leave the location. It is a nice idea at this time to repeat to them the intent of the meditation to remember as they return to a normal state of consciousness, such as, "Remember, you are a creative being, and your creative spirit is guiding you." Then you can use one of several methods to formally end the meditation and ask them to return to being present in the current time and place. If you had them count backward at the start of the meditation, you may have them count forward to the designated special number. If you chose another grounding and relaxation method at the start, you can reverse it, or simply ring a meditation chime or bell a few times or play a singing bowl, and then ask them to open their eyes when they are ready. This reversal of sorts or mirroring of parts of the opening procedure also serves as a nice post-meditation grounding, which I mentioned as an option earlier in the outline.

Something to keep in mind while creating your meditation is the length of time you want it to last. Remember, the length of the script on paper for a guided meditation will not be a good indicator of how long it will take to conduct the meditation from start to finish. This is because you do not read a guided meditation in the same manner you would read a nonfiction article or a fictional story out loud. When you read a guided meditation, you need to incorporate pauses. Pausing allows the participants experiential time. If you ask them to visualize a temple and then race on to the next line, they will have no time to visualize anything. Timing is very important and will take practice. It is a good idea to find a friend who is willing to serve as a test subject for the content of your guided meditation and your meditation-conducting skills. Be open to their constructive criticism.

Of course, if you are conducting a guided meditation with a group or another person live before a ritual, an initiation, a Reiki attunement, or some other event, you can read the script aloud to them. However, what if you need to send the script to a friend, student, or coven mate for later use, or you want to use it for yourself? Simply record yourself reading it aloud and then use the recording! Don't forget to physically set the tone and create sacred space in your environment beforehand or to instruct those who will use the meditation to do so.

Guided meditations can be a wonderful multipurpose tool for solo practitioners, teachers, covens, public gatherings, and groups of all sizes. They can powerfully harness intent and create a cohesive group and a nurturing environment. With a little practice and pre-planning, it is both easy and fun to create a guided meditation that is custom-tailored to your needs. Be empowered! Go forth and create your own meditative experiences.

Blake Octavian Blair *is an eclectic Pagan, ordained minister, shamanic practitioner, writer, Usui Reiki Master-Teacher, tarot reader, and musical artist. Blake blends various mystical traditions from both the East and West along with a reverence for the natural world into his own brand of modern Neo-Paganism and magick. Blake holds a degree in English and Religion from the University of Florida. He is an avid reader, crafter, and practicing vegetarian. Blake lives with his beloved husband, an aquarium full of fish, and an indoor jungle of houseplants. Visit him on the Web at www.blake octavianblair.com or write him at blake@blakeoctavianblair.com.*

Illustrator: Rik Olson

Smudge Plants and How to Use Them

Charlie Rainbow Wolf

Using herbs and incense in ceremonies or rituals is practiced by members of diverse cultures and belief systems, although many people may associate smudging with Native American customs. Smudging can take all sorts of forms, from the sticks that can be purchased in many metaphysical shops to simply sprinkling loose herbs over a fire source, such as a charcoal briquette. Some herbs are more suited to a particular way of preparation. For example, sweetgrass is usually braided. Sage and lavender are good herbs to tie

into bundles, while the needles of evergreens lend themselves to being sprinkled into a fire.

The fire that lights the smudge can also vary from tradition to tradition. Sometimes the smudge is lighted from the ritual fire. If this is not possible, I've seen a cinder from a previous ritual fire added to whatever flame is burning so that it becomes a ritual fire. It may be appropriate to light the smudge from ceremonial candles, or to take an ember from the sacred fire and place it in a heatproof receptacle so that the herbs might be offered to it. There's really no right or wrong way to smudge. It depends largely on the traditions and the ceremony being observed, but mostly on the intent with which the smudging ritual is performed.

Many people associate smudge bowls with the abalone shell, or paua shell. These shells are useful and pretty, and while some practices favor this, others say it is an insult to the spirit of the shell to mar its iridescent face with the scorch that the smudge heat can leave. The shells can get very hot when holding the smudge, and some kind of carrier or heat shield is advised. I've seen people cradle shells and other smudge pots in antlers, as a carrier. Smudge bowls don't have to be shell. They can be ceramic dishes, cast-iron cauldrons, or just about anything else that is fireproof and fits in with the ritual being done.

While the herbs lend the magical or healing energy to the smudge, it's the actual smoke, not the fire, that is used in a smudging ceremony—and smudge can create a lot of smoke, very quickly sometimes! The smudge is meant to smolder, not blaze. The rising smoke is said to carry the energy of the ceremony up to the spirits. Some people use a special feather or bird wing to fan the herbs and direct the smoke, while others use an actual fan. Generally, the smoke is passed around the area to be cleansed or the person to be healed, using the fan to make sure that all the necessary areas of the space or the person have been exposed to the smudge. Some smudge mixes can even be inhaled, so that the person has been smudged inside and out; but if you are uncertain of what is in the mixture or how you might physically react, this is something that is best avoided.

Lighting the smudge for ritual use is one thing, but extinguishing it once the ceremony is over is quite another. In many traditions, it is disrespectful to the fire elementals to use water to extinguish any flame. Braids and bundles will eventually go out on their own. If you need to smother the smudge for any reason, then braids and bundles can be stubbed out, or suffocated in a pot of sand. If your smudge is in a smudge pot or bowl, stirring it with a stick (being careful not to catch the stick on fire!) will often help it burn out quickly. Dirt or sand could be placed over the herbs to smother them, too, but be careful if you choose to do this. They may still quietly smolder.

Smudging Plants

Now that you have an idea of the purpose of your smudge, your smudge pot, and your flame source, it's time to consider the plants you're going to use in your smudge.

Sage

When people think of smudging, they usually think of white sage, *Salvia apiana*. This is different from the culinary sage, *Salvia officinalis*. I do know people who smudge with the latter, simply because they can grow it in their own sacred space, rather than having to purchase something that is not indigenous. Once again, it's the intent that makes the magic.

White sage is sometimes called sweet sage, bee sage, or sagebrush. Botanically, the latter really refers to a species of Artemisia (*Artemisia ludoviciana*) rather than Salvia, but the misnomer is used in common language all the same. White sage is a scrubby bush that grows around the edges of the desert in the far Southwest. It's prized for the sweet aroma that it releases when crushed or burned.

Another sage that is sometimes used in the smudge ceremony is *Artemisia tridentata*, sometimes called desert sage, or black sage because it has black seeds, though it can be called white sage or sagebrush, too. Combining the two different sages, Artemisia and Salvia, can create a wonderful smudge that is cleansing, aromatic, and purifying. All sages fall under the rulership of Jupiter, the planet of expansion, hope, and potential.

White sage can be purchased tied in bundles or sticks or in loose form. It's just a matter of preference. Sage is considered to be a cleansing and purifying herb by many people. In folk magic throughout the world, sage is used to clear negative energies from buildings and other areas, either before ritual purposes or perhaps for more mundane reasons, like wanting to rid a new house of the energies of its previous occupants. When you smudge a person, it is said to cleanse the aura. This is why people are often smudged with sage before ceremonies or before entering into sacred space. Some people use sage to smudge themselves in the morning to clear the residue of the previous day from their energy field and prepare themselves for the day ahead.

Sweetgrass

Sweetgrass (*Hierochloe odorata*) is another well-known plant used in smudge. Sweetgrass is found more in the Midwest region of the United States than in the West, where the white sage grows. This plant has a sweet, almost vanilla-like smell, which it releases when it is burned or crushed. Sweetgrass is often burned with sage for grounding and protection. It is said to attract good energies and is sometimes used during invocations. It's been my experience that the sweetgrass is lit after the sage has been used; the sage purifies the area, and then the sweetgrass invites in the friendly and helpful energies.

CEDAR

Cedar is another common ingredient in smudge. Any type of cedar can be used. The most popular is probably the red cedar (*Thuja occidentalis*) or perhaps California cedar (*Libocedrus decurrens*). In many traditions, cedar is said to hold the spirits of the ancestors. It also is a purifier and releases a fresh odor when bruised or set alight. Cedar does the job of cleansing and also attracts positive energies, which makes it a wonderful addition to any smudge mixture. It's easiest to burn cedar loose over charcoal, although it can be tied with sage in a smudge stick or wand.

TOBACCO

Many people wouldn't think of adding tobacco (*Nicotiana tabacum*) to a smudge mix, but it has its uses here, as well as in the sacred pipe. In some traditions, tobacco is only to be used by men, as it is said that its medicine—or its energy—is too strong and fiery for a woman. It's true that natural tobacco does demand respect due to the high levels of nicotine and other substances in it. For smudging purposes, only wild or untreated tobacco should be used. Many believe it is tobacco that opens the door between our world and the spirit world, and this is why it is included in the smudge mix.

COMFREY

Just as tobacco was considered to be a man's herb, comfrey (*Symphytum officinale*) was considered to be the women's equivalent in some cultures, who used it in their smoking mixtures and for other purposes in many of the same ways that men used tobacco. Comfrey is another herb that brings protection to a smudge mixture. Comfrey can also assist in the desire for good health, making it an excellent addition to a healing ceremony.

Lavender

Sprigs of lavender can be bundled into a stick, or the flower heads can be used as a loose smudge on a glowing coal. English lavender (*Lavandula angustifolia*) is probably the easiest to obtain, but others are just as appropriate to use in smudge. Lavender brings a calming and peaceful energy to a smudge mix, as well as a sweet floral fragrance. Lavender also assists in opening the door for helpful spirits and energies to enter.

Mint

Are you surprised to see mint here? Don't be. There are so many different types of mint, each one slightly different and with something unique to offer. My favorites are lemon balm (*Melissa officinalis*), peppermint (*Mentha × piperita*), spearmint (*Mentha spicata*), and chocolate mint (*Mentha × piperita* 'Chocolate Mint'). Mint is protective, refreshing, and aromatic. It's inclusion in a smudge blend is both stimulating and calming, interestingly enough. The smell of mint is invigorating and beneficial when high-energy work is being done, but the actual vibration of mint is quite calming and soothing, and can help to calm those who are nervous or a bit too excitable. Mint is excellent for inclusion in healing blends, too, because of its wide range of curative properties.

Fennel

Fennel is another herb that you probably did not expect to see in an article on smudging, but once again, it's a fabulous inclusion. I'm partial to bronze fennel (*Foeniculum vulgare*), but any fennel is suitable. The leaves can be tied into the stick or used in loose smudge. Fennel has a smell a bit like anise or licorice, and is used to help banish negative energies. It is said to help build courage in men and aid with fertility in women.

ROSE

Rose petals are a nice inclusion in a loose mix. They're rather hard to tie into bundles, although this is not impossible for those who are patient. I favor the hip rose (*Rosa rugosa*) in my smudge blends simply because I find the petals the most fragrant. The energy of the rose is both compassionate and protective. Adding rose to a smudge mix also adds healing and balance to the energies. Roses have long been considered sacred to the goddesses, and are symbols of love and beauty.

Gathering Your Own Smudging Herbs

You can gather many of your own herbs for smudging if you are fortunate enough to live in a place where you can grow or harvest them. The best time for gathering herbs for smudge—or for any other purpose—is early in the morning, after the dew has gone but before the sun gets too hot. If you are harvesting herbs for smudge sticks, then take cuttings that are the same length of the stick you want to make. Use a sharp knife or a pair of scissors and make a clean cut, to do as little damage to the parent plant as possible. Be respectful; you're gathering magical items from a living organism for magical purposes. There are many who believe that the magic and the ceremony actually begin with the gathering of herbs, and they leave an offering of tobacco as a sign of respect and appreciation.

Once you have harvested your herbs, they need to be dried. I know some people who hang the herbs to dry and then bundle them. This does allow the herbs to dry more thoroughly, but it can make it harder to tie the bundles together. I usually use a method somewhere in the middle. I gather the herbs and tie the bundles together at the cut point. Then I hang them upside down outside, where they can catch both the sun and the breeze to help them dry. (I was told that hanging them upside down prevented the magic from running out, but I think someone was just trying to humor me. It does, however, help to keep the sap in the plant, rather than possibly dripping out of the cut stem.) I check the bundles often, and I bind them when they have started to dry nicely but before they get too brittle. I use a plant-based twine in a neutral color, although I have friends who tie

the bundles in colors of string chosen to reflect the purpose of the smudge stick. Do what feels right to you.

. . . .

There is much more to the smudge ceremony than what people might think. It is not just a way to purge the energies or prepare the participants; it is a powerful way to connect to all four elements. Should you choose to use an abalone shell, it will connect you to the element of water; the smoke connects with air, the flame with fire, and the smudge to earth. Smudging can help bring you into balance, prepare for an event, set the mood for the day, or assist in magical or healing work. Whether you're cleansing an area, working on healing magic, or simply looking for something to add to your daily devotional, there's a lot to be said for the sagacity in the sacred smoke.

Charlie Rainbow Wolf *is happiest when she's creating something, especially if it can be made from items that others have cast aside. She is passionate about writing and is deeply intrigued by astrology, tarot, runes, and other divination oracles. Knitting and pottery are her favorite hobbies, although she happily confesses that she's easily distracted by all the wonderful things that life has to offer. Charlie is an advocate of organic gardening and cooking, and lives in the Midwest with her husband and her special needs Great Danes. Visit her at www.charlierainbow.com.*

Illustrator: Jennifer Hewitson

Written in Stone: An Ancient Tool in a Modern World

Lexa Olick

The use of stones in modern-day Witchcraft keeps us deeply connected to our past. Large rocks such as boulders may initially seem powerful due to their size, but even the tiniest of stones can hold the strongest of meanings. Whether used for personal adornment, private purposes, or in public spaces, stones have always played an important role throughout our history. When we take a stone into our hands, we can immediately feel its physical characteristics, such as shape, weight, depressions, and surface texture, but the history behind the stone remains secret unless we do a bit of research.

Stones and rocks are best known for their long-lasting abilities as tools and building supplies. Sandstone specifically is a stone that resists weathering but at the same time remains easy to carve. Those are the qualities that make it an important decorative and practical building material. Of course, it has significant metaphysical properties as well.

We currently have endless uses for stones, some of which mimic those seen in nature. Rock wrens have been known to build their nests deep inside rock crevices, sometimes made of sandstone, to protect and hide their homes. However, even the nests themselves are composed of stones. Mud, twigs, and weeds are common building supplies for bird nests, but rock wrens utilize an impressive number of small stones to further strengthen their homes. The remarkable thing about these nests is that they even have a tiny walkway of pebbles that lead to the entrance. This most likely occurs when the birds drop the tiny stones as they drag them back home to complete their nests.

Every stone has magical properties. Just as a stone pathway can lead to the entrance of a wren's nest, sandstone is a stone of revealing truth. It is also used to build and strengthen relationships, which should come to no surprise since it's a very durable substance. The various colors make it a great building material, and the harder-to-detect shades add extra protection to a wren's home. The birds know where to look and can easily find their way back while still remaining undetected by predators.

While we still enjoy stone and dirt paths, some of our walkways have evolved into a method of public recognition. Engraved, personalized bricks are displayed to acknowledge good deeds. These bricks transform every step we take into a memorable tribute. The engravings usually distinguish those who support a cause or commemorate someone for their service, such as the bricks at the National WWII Museum in New Orleans. Something as simple as a walkway is transformed into a beautiful, long-lasting memorial. Public recognition through personalized bricks is a current method of documenting the kindly acts of others.

Stones document the oldest existence of human activity. One of the most remarkable things about primitive stone tools is that their function was often represented by their shape. For example, sharp edges represented cutting tools and arrowheads represented tools for hunting. There was a physical resemblance to the function the tool signified, which is an attribute also seen in magic wands.

Wands are commonly tipped with crystals, which is not only aesthetically pleasing, but very symbolic as well. Anyone who is familiar with crystallography, or at least has a good search engine on hand, can easily recognize a stone's individual importance; but even a wand lacking a stone can have meaning defined by its shape. While crystals are the most popular addition to a wand, acorns are also quite common. Priapic wands receive their name from Priapus, a god of fertility and livestock. He is usually depicted with an erect, oversized penis, which is an obvious symbol of fertility. Wands are generally phallic in

appearance and represent the male energy. Chalices and cauldrons have female energy, so visual anatomical symbolism is evident in these tools. The use of symbolism balances male and female energies during a ritual.

Wands are usually sentimental items and can represent a part of our personality. While they may be used in front of others, they are typically only handled by their owner. Therefore, they can be viewed as both public and private items.

During the Renaissance, pieces of jewelry were also seen as both public and private items. They were considered private because the small stones were intimately placed against the body, yet they were also public because they were visible for all to see. As head coverings gradually disappeared, this allowed jewels to be delicately woven into the hair. Necklines were lowered, which enabled necklaces and pendants to become fashionable. Even protective amulets were worn around the neck instead of being placed inside pockets and pouches. Amethyst was a common stone to use in protective amulets because the carved amethyst was also used to emphasize beauty, so it was able to be worn for its magical and aesthetical properties.

Emerald crosses were worn because their shape declared the wearer's religious faith and the stones also repelled evil spirits and illnesses. These are two stones that are still popular today.

Jewelry was above all a display of wealth. Jewels were noticeable signs of the riches found in the New World. Jewelry worn over a person's heart was a symbol of loyalty and devotion, especially portrait jewelry. Queen Elizabeth would give gifts of portrait jewelry, usually cameos, to seal more important relationships. The gesture would be acknowledged by the receiver by actively wearing the jewelry. This act of giving and accepting jewelry became a recognizable statement of loyalty.

Lockets are still a popular form of portrait jewelry today. They are also very intimate items that are meant to keep loved ones close. They hold a private memory, which is publicly displayed around the neck. The contents of the locket may be secret if it's kept closed, but even a closed locket is a recognizable item of significance.

Many modern-day lockets can be infused with essential oils or hold small trinkets inside their compartments. Some even hold small stones. Stones have always been a unique accessory because they tell a story. They hold sentimental value about when and where they came from. A stone's shape and texture can identify what sort of environment it originated from, but it's our memory of how we came to collect these stones that truly makes these pieces special.

The following project gives you the opportunity to embellish a stone that holds personal associations. The final result can remain hidden in a drawer or proudly displayed. The stone can become a tribute to a past memory, a small icon to honor nature, or even a gift. Whatever you choose, your rock will be adorned to accentuate its beauty.

Beaded Rock Art

This project uses beads to embellish natural elements, such as stones, feathers, and plants. The beads reflect the light and add a hint of sparkle to the stone's rough surface. Wrapped around the stone, the beads also outline its natural shape. The use of beads, feathers, and stones together creates a combination of rough and smooth textures.

Dried flowers and feathers adorn the stone. They're held tightly inside a beaded band. This is a simple project that appeals to our love of nature.

Gather the following supplies:

- A small stone, about 1½ to 3 inches in size

- Warm water and dish soap, to cleanse the stone

- Dried flowers

- Small feathers

- Tacky glue

- A size 12 beading needle

- Thread

- Some size 11 glass seed beads

- A toothpick

STEP ONE

Thoroughly clean the stone with warm water and dish soap, then set it aside to dry. Flat, oval stones work best for this project. If possible, I suggest collecting stones from a beach.

Step Two

If you are only interested in a beaded stone, then you can skip to step three. If you want to decorate your stone with dried flowers and feathers, place them flat against the front of the stone. You can arrange them as desired, but they should be placed more toward the top of the stone. If necessary, trim the bottoms of any long stems so they all fit on the stone. Once you are sure that all the flowers and feathers can fit nicely, apply a small amount of tacky glue to the ends and attach them to the front of the stone.

Step Three

Thread the needle and knot the end of the thread. Affix the knot to the back of the stone with tacky glue. Attach it toward the top of the stone, but leave enough space so the top of the stone will still be visible when the beading is complete. For example, if you are working on a three-inch stone, attach the thread one inch away from the top.

That way, you will have an inch of stone visible from the top, an inch of beading in the middle, and an inch of stone at the bottom. For a smaller stone, you can leave a space equal to the width of your slimmest finger.

STEP FOUR

Use your needle to pick up beads and string them onto your thread. We're using size 11 glass seed beads because they are large enough to handle without difficulty but still small enough that they will allow the stone to lie flat once the project has been completed.

Use a toothpick to apply an even line of glue across your stone. Carefully press your beaded thread against the glue. Continue to spiral the beads around the stone, and apply glue as necessary until the middle of your stone is covered.

STEP FIVE

Knot the end of your thread and glue it down against the back of the stone. You can try to hide the string by pushing it between the beaded layers with your needle.

The glue will still be tacky, so use your toothpick to even out the beading if necessary. Once satisfied, place the stone on its back to dry.

Lexa Olick *is the author of* Witchy Crafts: 60 Enchanted Projects for the Creative Witch. *She has previously contributed to other Llewellyn almanacs, such as the* Herbal Almanac *(2013), the* Witches' Companion *(2014), and the* Sabbats Almanac *(2015). She is a graduate of the University of Buffalo, where she studied art and art history. When she is not writing or crafting, she spends her time traveling, gardening, and adding to her collection of antique glassware. She currently lives in New York with her family and several hyperactive pets.*

Illustrator: Tim Foley

Magickal Monikers

Emyme

Pagan, Wiccan, Druid, Native American, and so on… You have stepped away from monotheistic religions and realized an affinity for an Earth-based belief system (EBBS) or spirituality. One integral part of the conversion process is creating/taking a spiritual name. This may be done at any step along the path. If it helps to take a name before immersion into all the intricacies, by all means do so. If it feels more comfortable to create a ritual and take a name at the end of an initiation period (perhaps a year and a day), that is also fine. EBBSs are wonderfully flexible; the comfort of the participant is of uppermost importance.

This practice of taking another name was most likely founded during the rise of those religions that chose to eliminate other religions perceived as pagan, heathen, heretical, and therefore "bad." It was infinitely safer to create a pseudonym in all dealings potentially dangerous to the health and welfare of the participants. Unfortunately, even here in the twenty-first century, the physical danger may still be quite real and present in certain parts of the world. In all societies, revealing spiritual preference and names remains a matter of choice. As an example, I choose to write under my Wiccan name, knowing my belief system may conflict with other aspects of my life. I am Emyme to my readers and someone else in my nine-to-five, Monday-through-Friday working life and my 24/7 home life.

I chose to create/discover my Wiccan name about two months into my year-and-a-day journey. Your name is out in the universe waiting for you to claim it. Without you realizing or knowing it, clues and hints have been set before you all of your life. Like lost pieces of a puzzle, it is up to you to find them and fit them together. Prior to setting out on an EBBS spiritual path, I was taught a method to learn the name of my guardian angel/protective spirit. I'm sure there are numerous processes that enable this discovery. What they all have in common is an underlying action with

> **Your name is out in the universe waiting for you to claim it. Without you realizing or knowing it, clues and hints have been set before you all of your life. Like lost pieces of a puzzle, it is up to you to find them and fit them together.**

open-minded, open-eyed perception, coupled with clear, honorable intention. You will know the name is right by a physical response. The physical reaction I had upon recognition of my angel name felt as though a pleasurable electric force had gone through my heart. Exactly the same feeling came over me when

my Wiccan name appeared on the paper, by my hand.

Here are several exercises and suggestions for the discovery/creation of your magickal name. I offer but a peek into the processes. When you discover the right name for you, further information is readily available online and in libraries. In the name of inclusion, I will refer to chosen names in this article as "spirit" names. I went about discovering or creating (whichever you prefer) my spirit name from several directions. Remember, this search is, in all ways, entirely about what makes you most comfortable.

The Request

This is the process that worked for me in discovering my angel, what I now think of as protective energy. It may be flexible enough to be revised and assist you in finding your own spirit name—just ask. That is correct—just ask. Ask the universe to show you your name. Literally say: "Please show me my spirit name, in many versions, in a way I will recognize, and give me a physical sign of recognition so I cannot misunderstand and I will be absolutely sure this is the right name." Ask over and over until you get the answer. Have no doubt that you will get an answer. I repeat: do not doubt, and you will get an answer. Remain patient, open, and watchful. Billboards, books, magazines, newspaper, the Internet, songs, movies, television...a name will begin to appear. It will pop up at odd times in different formats. It will be insistent until you get it, and when you get it, you will know it.

Numerology

There are many different charts available that assign numbers to the letters of the alphabet. The illustration is a pie chart with twenty-six equal divisions. One can also equate zero with the letter A, which adds one, making twenty-seven possible numbers. This is one of the first and most basic codes, still in use today. Due to its simplicity, it is a code that is easy to break. Therefore it has become more of a game or an amusing pastime.

Using the letters in your given name, add together the corresponding numbers and reduce them to a single digit to find the letter associated with that name. As an example, let's find the letters associated with the given name of Ann Smith:

A = 1, N = 14, N = 14
1 + 14 + 14 = 29
2 + 9 = 11
1 + 1 = 2
2 = B

S = 19, M = 13, I = 9, T = 20, H = 8
19 + 13 + 9 + 20 + 8 = 69
6 + 9 = 15
1 + 5 = 6
6 = F

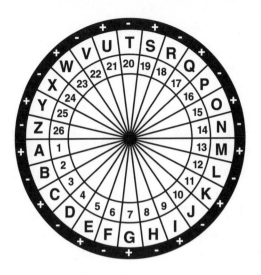

So the result is "BF." You might be able to see a word in those two letters or to use those two letters as the start of a more intricate word.

Going in the opposite direction on the wheel, you can use the numbers in your birth date, using A = zero. Here is an example:

May 23, 1954
05 – 23 – 1954 = A E B C A I E D

Again, you might be able to create a word out of those letters. I played with the number of letters in my given name and matched the totals to letters of the alphabet, then did the same with the totals of my birth date, with and without the "19" (as in 1955). Unfortunately, neither one was really usable. Nothing really struck me. However, this method may work for you.

Glyphs

Glyphs mean many different things to different people. They can be pictures from ancient carvings, or have a purpose in the computer world far beyond my comprehension. Here I wish to address an incredibly simple use of the glyph. Write out your name. You can use your first name only, last name only, middle name only, or your entire name. Now cross out every vowel. Next take all of the consonants and pile them onto one another to create a symbol. Obviously, this type of spirit name or symbol is not meant to be spoken—think "The Artist Formerly Known as Prince." However, this choice may the one that rings in your heart.

Name-Generating Websites

At www.namegeneratorfun.com, you will find a collection of name generators that may help you discover your spirit name. You can use these to find your vampire name, hobbit name, elf name, etc. Even if none of those options call to you, they are entertaining. You may find some part of a name that becomes a jumping-off point for your own spirit name.

This quest proved rather merry. My favorite fairy name is as follows, using my first and last names:

Meadow Quillfrost: She watches over the birds. She lives in fields…

These next two fairy names are fun, but are not quite how I see my fey self. The first one uses my middle and last names:

Briar Vinewitch: She brings couples together. She lives in leafy dells…

The second fairy name uses my first and middle names:

Buttercup Jupiterfilter: She is mysterious and secretive…

After the fairy name, the mermaid name felt most right and was the most interesting to me. Here is mine:

Red Cavern Fish (curalium caverna): Typically the tail and fins are an unusually deep red colour acting as a camouflage from predators…

At times it was a little disconcerting to see the similarities among the different names chosen. Both my fairy and mermaid names show me in red, which is not a hue I would have expected.

The elf name generator gave the most options and the opportunity to create a unique name (and perhaps one that is difficult to pronounce—Elvish is a tricky language to master) by using different prefixes and suffixes. Of all options presented, I chose the distinctive name of *Thurilosteth*, which translates to "Empty Secret."

Here is a sampling of my other potential names:

Pirate name: *Calico Mary Rackham*

Shakespeare name: *Calpurnia Guildentstern*

Dragon name: *Magor the Ash Maker*

While this was a fun way to spend some time, certainly none of these resonated as my spirit name.

Personal Totems

Do you identify with a particular animal, feel connected to a specific insect, or have an affinity for one type of bird? (Should you still be searching for your spirit critter, there are *many* articles on the Web about discovering your animal.) My spirit animal is the chipmunk, and ladybugs have featured prominently in my life. I have incorporated them into my personal coat of arms; however, both of them felt too cute to be my spirit name.

Is there a flower, plant, herb, or tree that holds great significance for you? My favorite flower is a yellow rose, followed by the sunflower. I love cinnamon, and I identify with holly. I considered the name Hollyrose, but there are many Holly Roses on Google and thus too much chance for confusion. (Google "Emyme" and you get a musical organization for young people in Europe—rather obscure.) Also

consider gems, precious stones, and metals. Although none of these options worked for me, do not discount them—try any and all ideas. You will know if the name is right.

Planetary/Celestial Influences

Examine your zodiac sign. Do you favor a particular planet, star, or moon? Do you identify with the story or qualities of a specific mythological figure? Is there a geographical area here on planet Earth that holds special meaning for you? In researching mythology, I came across the story of the demigoddess Io, one of the many conquests of Zeus. She is also the figure for whom the Ionian Sea is named, and one of the moons of the planet Jupiter (another name for Zeus) is named for her. I am a Taurus, and Io was changed into a cow—a bovine connection there. Goddess, moon, sea—all in one neat package. I honor Io with a handcrafted, one-of-a-kind figurine and include her name in one of my easy-to-remember computer passwords. Although she holds a special place in my spirit life, I chose to leave her out of my spirit name.

Pet Names or Nicknames

Nicknames may be grounded in basic truths, such as Peewee = short, Junior = named for a parent, Ace = baseball pitcher, or Fish = a swimmer. Nicknames may be given to you by someone else, or they may be chosen by you if you believe your given name is wrong somehow. While exploring this option, I felt I was finally getting closer to finding my spirit name. To a chosen few, I am "Emma," which comes from my first and middle initials, M and A. This name resonated with me, but I craved something unique. "Emme" is too common. On to the next alternative.

Language Arts

You can use backward writing, acronyms, anagrams, or palindromes to find your spirit name. Let's use the name Ann Smith as an example.

Ann Smith = Htims Nna, or perhaps Thims Nan, or Nan Thims, or Thin Mans. AS or SA.

Don't be discouraged—your name may be a better fit for these techniques than poor Ann's. Part of the pleasure is in the search.

I love palindromes, which is when a word reads the same forward or reversed. After working for some time with all the letters of my name and the numbers in my date of birth, I began to play with versions of "Emma" and "me" and "mine" and "my"... and EMYME appeared. There it was on paper in black and white. There is a special physical feeling when you find the right name, and this feeling settled into my heart on seeing this name. I have yet to decide how to pronounce it, as so far I only use it in print. Your choice may also come with this quandary. When the time comes and a decision is required, the universe will let its intentions be known.

As you can see, the choices are quite numerous. I have no doubt barely scratched the surface. There is no right or wrong name; rest assured you will know it when you find the perfect spirit name. In the quest for a magickal moniker, I wish you delightful searching and exultant discovery.

Emyme *practices as a solitary eclectic in the wilds of southern New Jersey. With an affinity for "power" bags and candle magick, she is currently researching Pennsylvania Dutch Braucherei talismans and charms. In addition to her Llewellyn contributions, she writes flash-fiction fairy-tale adaptations. Owned by two cats, Stars and Shadow, she is a proud mother, daughter, sister, aunt, and niece. Emyme can be reached at catsmeow24@verizon.net.*

Illustrator: Kathleen Edwards

Recognizing and Combating the Evil Eye: Putting It On and Poking It Out

Esthamarelda McNevin

Have you ever unknowingly had an enemy who intended to do you actual personal harm? Do you know someone who is bitter and magical enough to twist the tides of fate into a tsunami of circumstances set abruptly against you? Has your self-esteem ever been obliterated under an unrelenting downpour of public scrutiny, while all those little hairs on the back of your neck stood witness like so many Druids on a beach? Perhaps you, too, have come under the deadly gaze of the evil eye.

This curse is employed when someone aspires to erode another person's confidence or sense of worth intentionally, by projecting emotions such as jealousy, envy, and greed. This hex gives our own fear and paranoia the opportunity to dig in deep and take hold of our psyche through passive-aggressive manipulation and sympathetic magic. If left helpless against the evil eye, we begin to believe in our worst fate, unintentionally empowering and manifesting the curse with our own judgments.

Dispel from your mind that image of an embittered Sicilian Mafioso launching a spittle of condemnation from beneath a floral taffeta halo of hate. After all, it's the ones we trust implicitly who most favor curses like the evil eye. These are people we often don't suspect, or those we think are incapable of subversive betrayal. Those who cast the evil eye are not the ones we see coming, but the people who get close, learn our weaknesses, and use this knowledge to exploit us for their personal gain.

Such use of this "covetous gaze" indicates that the hexer not only wants what *you* have—be it physical wealth, emotional happiness, or esoteric gifts—but also wants you *not to have it*. If you have been victim to this phenomenon, which numerous cultures recognize and combat, take comfort in knowing that you are not alone. Predatory sympathetic magic like the evil eye is one of the oldest and most primal curses on the books. The *Greek Magical Papyri* is evidence enough of how favored this hex truly was in the ancient world. Our surviving recipes from the Greek Hellenistic period document a primordial penchant for sacrificial spells and rare animal talismans, evocative proof of Paganism's deep-rooted models of mystical survivalism, which drove countless devotees to extreme Gnostic acts for the sake of self-protection.

Long before the Wiccan Rede gave us the "An it harm none…" mandate, our ancient Pagan ancestors were prone to hexing the piss 'n' vinegar out of each other, because they saw magic as just another aspect of daily social survival. In fact, the evil eye has such a long history of use that it's credited with inspiring protective artwork, amulets, tonics, ethereal cures, and alchemical remedies, a great many of which have survived since antiquity. Counter and reverse techniques have crossed cultures and continents under the guise of liberal folk bohemia or simply as gypsy luck, and are still very much in use today. If nothing else, the antidotes for the evil eye act as a form of psychological relief. While problem-solving such a magical battle of wills, the victim often chooses to withdraw into solitary meditation or pursue the hexer's *own* weak surrender, as a countermeasure against the curse. The evil eye exists, and it is viewed across the world as a vehicle of prejudice and hate. Many esoteric traditions believe that we must

guard ourselves daily against attack or we risk falling prey to the energies afoot.

Primal sympathetic magic makes sense in a lot of biological ways, especially when we consider that mating and professional competition among our social groups often expose our instinctually reactive emotions.

The sociological studies of academics like Carl Jung relate these emotional outbursts to our deeply rooted psychological struggle between acceptance and intolerance as social mammals. Our darker, more primal and survivalistic emotions constantly challenge our rational civic goodness, tempting our impulse to respond to situations of public distress with fight-or-flight instincts of survivalism. Like all curses, the evil eye is a social and psychological weapon employed by an aggressor to trigger a fear response in the target.

When acquaintances plot our failure, a deep loss of hope and an increase in personal shame are constant stepping stones on the descending path of spiritual deprivation. This is because curses like the evil eye will sustain the hexer's subtle predatory advantage as they sabotage happiness, innocence, and good luck from the lives of others. Those who have cast the curse find the results addictive, and those who have endured this type of hex know all too well that attracting the primal disdain of another human is no laughable super-stition. Eyeballs involved or not, we are a territorial and superstitious species of instinctively driven emotional beings, sometimes willing to trust or hate others irrationally and to our own disadvantage.

Too many people suffer the emotional effects of common antiso-cial behaviors like bullying, taunting, and public displays of rejection. Let's face it: the evil eye is everywhere, and we all instinctively know how to use it. One does not have to sit down and cast a spell in order to cast the evil eye. Moreover, we are all sitting ducks; as social mam-mals, we really just want to be liked and accepted for who we are. As a global society, public opinion matters more to us now than it ever has, which is why getting "the evils" from someone can be so off-putting.

Why is this primordial hex so powerful? Whether we like it or not, our feeling of social acceptance is a determinate factor in the vast ma-jority of our lifestyle decisions; this is especially the case with choices concerning appearance, marriage, and career, as well as drug or alco-hol use. We may feel socially valued and praised when we look and act like our colleagues, friends, or families. We may feel a sense of comfort in following long-held models of human social conformity. This means that when we are truly hexed with dark, antisocial magic like the evil eye, it is often accompanied by unethical slander, hidden jokes at our expense, or various other forms of social humiliation. This type of black magic is a pressing social issue in our modern com-munities because, like so many of us, the evil eye has gone digital.

No app, trash bin, or delete button can erase harsh social judg-ments once we have received them; it's up to *us* to problem-solve, take an objective perspective, and process social disagreements. We must defend ourselves mentally and spiritually against negative action di-rected at us, especially when it becomes clear that no resolution is feasible. Even blocking the individual from our contact information may not stop truly malicious social behaviors. The people who use negative psychological magic rely on the emotional responses we experience when we feel targeted, embarrassed, or shamed by others in public: this is what the original evil-eye hex accomplishes best.

Don't lose heart, dear readers; after all, it is the act of doing something about hexes that gets them out of our spiritual aura and off our minds. Most religions have long recognized the psychological effects of negative sympathetic magic like the evil eye and have developed charms, talismans, prayers/mantras, and spiritual prescriptions to combat them. All human cultures have their own techniques to help remove the effects of black magic from one's astral, physical, and mental space uniformly.

These methods and their various tools are designed to help us remember how to overpower evil with constant mindfulness on all planes of reality. Like the superstitions that they combat, the true power of these unhexing practices is in the effect they have on our *own* problem-solving and social-reasoning skills. Some of these practices might seem extreme or exact in their approach, but this older form of detail-oriented magic removes the problem from the psyche by using one extraordinary spell ingredient or talisman at a time. Moreover, anti-hex prescriptions like daily prayer or amulet jewelry can improve our mental focus and attention span, giving us a feeling that we are counteracting or repelling any negativity that might come our way simply by reminding us to think of our own protection and etheric shields throughout the day.

When it comes to casting the evil eye, most cultural traditions believe in the "keep it secret, keep it safe" model in order to test loyalties and save face. This means that malicious whispering, hissing, and cursed-gift giving are the main ways that one comes under the gaze of this curse. Abrahamic cultures like Judaism, Christianity, and Islam all have daily prayers and genuflect traditions that use mnemonic prayer and physical gestures like kneeling or making the sign of the cross to dispel malignant energies. This method of constant vigilance is exhausting for those not born into it, but as with all prayer, repetition breeds nostalgia.

For natural and animistic cultures like Hinduism and Buddhism, as well as some modern fusion Pagan practices, the evil eye is a black hole of bad karma that must be treated with right action, with prayer, and sometimes by taking a sacred pilgrimage. The prevailing belief and strategy in many of these traditions is to transform the self and make peace with the karma of having cultivated an enemy. The largely nonviolent spiritual traditions of Asia all teach that we are meant to evolve into our own karma. This means that we can neither wrestle nor play victim with our fate, but are instead encouraged to rise to the challenge.  Folk charms and auspicious symbols are used everywhere in Asian culture to inspire this proactive response to esoteric problems. Each painted wall, hand-stitched garment, or item of crafted jewelry can consequently become a vehicle for either evoking a positive manifestation or dispelling the evil eye.

Human culture is a vast and diverse landscape bound inextricably to a binary causal system of life and death. We can take this social competition to extremes when caught up in the frenzy of creation. Like any hex that is detected, the evil eye requires attention and spiritual protection, speaking to an even greater need to renew bonds of trust and loyalty *only* with those who earn it. For anyone left in question, here is a quick guide to the many spiritual techniques used to put on and gouge out the evil eye.

Amulets That Will Rid You of the Evil Eye

Ruby jewelry, blue and green nazar beads, hand of Fatima charms, hemsa (or hamsa) charms, hand of Miriam charms, jutti shoe charms, Brigid's cross charms, pentacle charms, blue jewelry, braided sweetgrass jewelry, Uli nana pono beads, Cabalistic Cross charms, Christian Cross charms, Seven African Powers charms, needle or sword charms.

Six Signs You Might Be Under the Gaze of the Evil Eye

1. A sudden and unexplainable fear of activities that once gave you great joy.

2. Nausea, lightheadedness, or weakened endurance when engaged in magic.

3. An overwhelming sense of anger or doom without reason or origin.

4. Hairs frequently standing on end (a sort of astral defense).

5. Feeling drawn into passive-aggressive or subtextual modes of communication.

6. Observing protracted looks or forced eye contact from overly responsive acquaintances.

Six Ways the Evil Eye Is Cast

1. Gifting cursed or hexed nazar beads or luck charms.

2. Spitting over the palm or between fingers in the direction of an enemy or directly upon their shadow, evoking a dark cloud over them.

3. A prolonged glance or moment of forced eye contact in which a look of deep hate or harmful intent is expressed.

4. Windows of one's car or home being vandalized.

5. Judgments, faults, or failures whispered beneath the breath while the victim is present (this affects the unconscious mind).

6. Crossing out the eyes of an enemy from all images or photos encountered.

Three Time-Tested and Proven Defense Tactics to Combat the Evil Eye

1. Daily prayer at sunrise and sunset, or upon waking and before bed.

2. A new and personally chosen amulet purchased from a healer and charged with the energy of a sacred place, which is worn as needed or daily until death; by British custom only to be burried by a loyal friend, family member, or coven member.

3. Eyeball symbols and protective charms hidden in seams and sewn into clothing, drapes, and bedding and drawn on windows, doors, and beds to protect the mind, body, and spirit.

PRINT RESOURCES

Cunningham, Scott. *Cunningham's Encyclopedia of Magical Herbs.* St. Paul, MN: Llewellyn Publications, 1985.

Greer, John Michael. *The New Encyclopedia of the Occult.* St. Paul, MN: Llewellyn Publications, 2003.

Jung, Carl G. *Man and His Symbols.* Garden City, NY: Doubleday, 1964.

Nock, Arthur Darby. "Greek Magical Papyri," *Journal of Egyptian Archaeology* 15 (1929).

The Quran. Oxford: Oxford University Press, 2004.

Tresidder, Jack. *The Complete Dictionary of Symbols.* San Francisco, CA: Chronicle, 2005.

Online Resources

Ancient Huna, www.ancienthuna.com/index.htm.

Jewish Gift Place, "What Is the Evil Eye," www.jewishgiftplace.com/What -is-the-Evil-Eye.html.

Lucky Mojo, "The Evil Eye," www.luckymojo.com/evileye.html.

Sacred Texts, "The Evil Eye," www.sacred-texts.com/evil/tee.

Esthamarelda McNevin (Missoula, MT) *is the co-founding Priestess and ceremonial oracle of Opus Aima Obscuræ, a nonprofit Pagan temple haus. She has served the Pagan community for fourteen years as an Eastern Hellenistic Priestess, freelance lecturer, author, artist, and poet. Estha studies and teaches courses on ancient and modern Pagan history, multicultural metaphysical theory, ritual technique, international cuisine, organic gardening, herbal craft, alchemy, and occult symbolism. In addition to hosting public rituals for the sabbats, Estha organizes annual philanthropic fundraisers, Full Moon spellcrafting ceremonies, and women's divination rituals for each Dark Moon. To learn more, please explore www.facebook. com/opusaimaobscurae.*

Illustrator: Bri Hermanson

Magical Transformations

Everything Old Is New Again

Big Magick for a Small World

Melanie Marquis

Our world is fraught with hunger, war, disease, oppression, pollution, and many other plagues caused largely or solely by humankind. As Pagans, many of us accept and welcome the role of stewards to the earth. We respect our planet and strive to protect her, heal her, and defend her to the best of our individual and collective abilities—only we don't always know where to start! There is conflict everywhere, sickness everywhere, abuse and suffering everywhere. We want to help, but what's a Witch to do when faced with a whole world of trouble?

It's hard to know where to concentrate our powers and how best to utilize those powers. While we don't doubt the possibility or even likelihood of magickal success when we're engaged in small-scale, everyday spellwork, when it comes to believing that our magick can literally save the world, doubt can crash down like a hammer and smash our usually unwavering faith to bits. I've been casting magick for years in attempts to end war, stop needless violence, end hunger, and free oppressed people, and while I've witnessed that such spells indeed have their effects, those effects fall far short of what is needed and desired. My spells to end war might result in a temporary ceasefire, or if I cast some magick to end hunger, I might hear news about a shipment of humanitarian aid. When I work a spell to cure the world of illness and infirmity, it might result in a new advance in medicine that carries hope for people with a disease or disability, but never does the spell do quite enough, and the effects are often ephemeral. That's not good enough. We want *lasting* results, *lasting* positive changes for our planet, and to do this, we need each other. We need more people believing in their abilities to perform such world-changing magick, and we need to all be applying our abilities in the most effective ways possible.

We want *lasting* results, *lasting* positive changes for our planet, and to do this, we need each other. We need more people believing in their abilities to perform such world-changing magick, and we need to all be applying our abilities in the most effective ways we can devise.

Casting such widespread magick is certainly challenging, but it's also certainly possible, and there are many techniques you can use to make your globally minded spellwork both easier and more effective.

I've identified several factors to take into consideration when planning and casting globally minded magick. These techniques can give your worldwide spells a better chance of working. Try them out, and hopefully you will be inspired to discover even more ways to overcome the challenges that prevent widespread magick from performing as well as it could. Together, we can do this, so let's do it! Here's what I've learned.

Big Magick Requires Big Power

Different spells require different amounts of magickal power. A spell is like a vehicle in which your intentions travel, and the energy you put into the spell is the fuel. If your spell isn't going very far or very fast, and if the aim of your spell is something that's fairly likely to happen anyway, even without magickal intervention, then you don't need a great deal of fuel to move it. In contrast, if your spell does need to traverse a long distance, or bring immediate results, or accomplish terrific miracles that would otherwise have a poor probability of occurring, then your spell will need more fuel to make it go.

When I'm merely smoothing and calming the energies of my home, for instance, I don't call on any spirits or powers other than my own. I just create within my own heart and mind the energy with which I want to fill the room, and I project that energy into the space. That sort of everyday magick—a quick and easy charm, in this case—doesn't need any especially tremendous power behind it. Anyone can do such magick with just a little practice and an awareness of the fact that we do indeed have this ability.

On the other hand, the spells I cast in an attempt to end wars, dispel oppressive world leaders, end animal poaching, clean the

oceans, and other grand aims that require ripping giant gaps in the fabric of space-time and then reweaving it skillfully and precisely, stitch by stitch—those spells require much more power than I personally hold. I can't help but feel a sense of futility when I do such heartfelt yet idealistic magick, and even though I try my best to overlook it and ignore it, there's an honest part of me that doubts the magick will succeed, knowing I can't possibly channel all the power I truly need for such workings all on my own.

For those "big" spells, we need all the help we can get. This extra power can be drawn from deities, spirits, and even the land itself. Call on energies that have a special association or connection to the target of your magick. For example, if you're casting a spell to protect whales, try calling on the very power of the ocean. If you're working a spell to help heal the ecosystems of Northern California, you might utilize the energies of Mount Shasta, a sacred site believed to radiate a powerful healing energy. Likewise, you might employ ley lines, regional deities, and spirits of the dead whose descendants dwell at the place in question.

You might also incorporate the power of the moon and the stars and other heavenly bodies, or tap into the energies residing deep down in the very core of the earth. When possible, anchor your spell to powerful natural features such as mountains, oceans, rock formations, and ancient trees, as doing so will help the magick stick around for as long as it takes to do its trick. Your magickally minded friends might be willing to help you, too, and as every individual has their own unique powers and abilities, having multiple people focused on accomplishing the same spell goal is a huge asset. All these energy sources can provide extra fuel for your extra-big magick so that it can truly work wonders.

Distance Matters, But You Can Travel It

Magick requires connection between the spell's caster and the spell's target. This connection is easy to forge if the object of your spell is right in front of you, but if the target of the magick is thousands of miles away, making that connection is a lot more challenging. Traditionally, magick was typically targeted to affect circumstances in one's own place, such as bringing more animals for the hunt, increasing the fertility of the land, or magnifying one's personal good fortune.

Today, our big world is more connected than ever before. Not only can we travel all the way around it, but we can also communicate via phone, post, and Internet with friends scattered all over the planet. In small-town America and big cities alike, we have access to goods crafted in faraway corners of the globe we'd probably seldom think of otherwise. In this highly connected world lies the potential for great magick—far-reaching magick that can affect not just our own place, but places all around our wide world.

We're used to using symbols in our magick to help forge the connections required for a successful spellcasting, but when we're looking to do some really big magick to affect some place at a great distance from us, those symbols need to be chosen more specifically and more carefully. For instance, if you want to work a spell to bring peace to a war-torn country, you could employ in your spell something obvious, like a peace symbol, but it won't really help you to traverse the great distance between yourself and the ravaged place in question. Instead, or in addition, choose symbols that are tied specifically to the target of the magick. In this example, you might use the country's flag, a map, or photos of the place. You might decide to create your own symbol for your spell target, complete with specific place names, specific names and photos of significant people in power,

state seals, military insignia, and other identifying words and images. Incorporating more exact, precise symbols of the area where your magick is targeted makes for a stronger connection that can allow your magick to cross oceans and move mountains.

You can also overcome the distance divide in magick with a little friendly international cooperation. Find friends or pen pals who live in different areas around the world, so that when you need to do a spell to affect one of those regions, you can mail to your buddy a physical object into which you've cast the spell, getting your magick physically closer to exactly where it needs to be.

Being On Time Is Important

Ordinary spellwork focused on small or medium-sized goals can usually succeed whether or not lunar phase and other aspects of astrological timing are heeded. Although it always *helps* to pay attention to such things and to harmonize your magick with the ever-changing rhythms of the universe, it's not always essential to do so. When your spell goals are very lofty, however, timing your magick as optimally as possible can give it that extra little nudge that can make all the difference.

Try working spells for manifestation, growth, and increasing positive energies when the moon is waxing, and save your binding spells and banishing magick for the waning moon. Take into consideration the planets as well. For instance, you might time your spells to coincide with particular planetary conjunctions, eclipses, meteor showers, and other stand-out astronomical events. If you notice Venus shining brightly, you might decide to incorporate the energies of that planet into your spell. Lasting, world-changing magick is difficult, and every extra fortification and fuel you can find for your spell will improve your chances for success. Try casting the following spells, and see what elements you might add to these general frameworks to make the magick even more powerful.

Spell to Stop the Worldwide War Machine

Work this spell to end wars at the time of the dark moon or during a lunar eclipse. Take an envelope and write on it "War Machine." Fill the envelope with symbols of the war machine, such as pictures, news clips, pieces of paper on which you've described specific leaders or political systems in detail, etc. Name names. Name weapons. Call on the old gods of the places in question to help you with your spell, call up the energies of the earth (making use of sacred places and ley lines

and such), call on the moon and the sun—any big power sources you wish to work with.

Roll the envelope up tightly, tie it up, and puncture it straight through with several nails—old rusty nails, if you can get them. As you do so, envision the war machine breaking down: see their guns all floppy and useless, hear in your head the announcement of a ceasefire, see the headlines announcing that traditional war is obsolete, see their bombs dismantled, see the oppressive leaders trapped and bound and miniscule, etc. Picture that whole mechanism of war and destruction as tiny, trapped, bound, useless, and unable to act. Say words to the same effect:

This war machine is trapped and bound. It can no longer exist. It can no longer act. I bind the guns. I bind the bombs. I bind the missiles.

I bind the perpetrators of the violence. They can no longer act. Their power is in my hands. Their power is mine. Their power is mine.

Then either bury the paper or seal it in a jar filled with fresh water and lavender or sage or another calming herb—or you could go another route and fill the jar with muddy water and broken glass or nails.

Spell to Bring Caring and Compassion to Power

Cast this spell when the moon is waxing and almost full, or when Venus is shining brightly in the morning or night sky. Hold a rock in your hand and say:

This is not a rock, but the loving, compassionate heart of creatures who crave peace that I hold in my hand.

Fill the rock with as much love and desire for peace as you can conjure, letting it flow from your heart into the stone.

Now get a dish of fresh water and fill it with herbs and energies of the aspects you feel our world needs more of—perhaps sage for wisdom, rose for love, lavender for peace, rosemary for friendship, mint for change and renewal, and so on. Place the rock in the dish of water for a while. Then leave the rock outside somewhere uncovered, in a sacred or extra-powerful place if possible, and envision its energies being connected to the very heart of the earth and to the cosmic bodies above. See this connection as a single thread of pulsating, positive energy, a bond that cannot be broken. Feel its strength, drawing from the powerful earth itself and radiating to the heavens above.

Pour the water in a circle around the rock, to further surround the peace lovers in a ring of protection, and also so that as the water evaporates, these energies will be dispersed to do their work. As you place the rock and pour out the water, affirm your intention by saying, "Caring and compassion, rise to power!" or something similar. Envision a more compassionate, caring world.

• • • • • • • • • • • •

These globally minded spells might seem too idealistic or optimistic, but the only way we'll know for sure is to try them. If we work together and apply our skills and knowledge as best we can, who knows? We might be able to save the world.

Melanie Marquis *is the author of* The Witch's Bag of Tricks *(Llewellyn, 2011) and* A Witch's World of Magick *(Llewellyn, 2014). She's the founder of United Witches global coven and also serves as local coordinator for Denver Pagan Pride. She's written for many Pagan publications, including* Circle Magazine, Pentacle Magazine, *and* Spellcraft. *A freelance writer, folk artist, Tarot reader, mother, and eclectic Witch, she's passionate about finding the mystical in the mundane through personalized magick and practical spirituality. Visit Melanie at www.facebook.com/melaniemarquisauthor or www.melaniemarquis.com or on Twitter @unitedwitches.*

Illustrator: Christa Marquez

Tower of Truth, Wall of Wonder: A Ritual to Heal a Painful Past

Natalie Zaman

When my daughter entered into her first romantic relationship, I expected there to be drama—but not from me. Watching her conjured up memories of myself at her age, and then…buckets of tears. Like so many people, I bear scars from my childhood that are still healing from the inside. Everyone has a story. Here's a bit of mine.

Ruins

When I was about ten years old, my dad left the family. I felt worthless after his departure; one parent had abandoned

me and the other seemed to blame me for it. I understand now that my father's actions had nothing to do with me, and my mother was hurt beyond reason, but back then I was desperate for love and acceptance. During my adolescence I made bad decisions, believing that taking reckless risks would win me the affection I craved.

Instead, I was bullied.

Assaulted.

And worse.

I became wary and fearful, and even though it didn't feel right to hide myself away, I felt safest in the shadows, so I stayed there for a long time.

I believe that we are the creators of our lives. Each time we incarnate, we choose the challenges we'll face, our souls growing and "getting it" a little more with each go-round. Remembering past hurts tipped me off that forgiveness of some kind was probably in order. I read many books, including Colin Tipping's *Radical Forgiveness*, and found myself in one of those "getting it" moments.

In recent years especially, I've tried very hard to always think positive. It makes sense, right? If you want good things to happen to you, think good thoughts! It's the "secret" behind *The Secret*, the "how-to" behind *How to Stop Worrying and Start Living*, and the "*Magic*" of *Believing*. A bit of Tipping's philosophy mirrored a part of my own that I'd neglected, that "we are spiritual beings having a human experience." To be human is to experience emotions—*all* of them.

While I still believe it's very important to have an optimistic outlook, I saw that in my desire to overcome a painful past, I'd stopped "feeling my feelings." The fear, doubt, and self consciousness that helped me survive as a teenager were holding me back as an adult. My creativity and self-confidence were shaken by the smallest setbacks, and the resulting anxiety and stress took a toll on my health. There was no such thing as "safe."

Watching my daughter enter what had been for me a traumatic time presented me with an opportunity to correct this. In her, I recalled my former self, but where I saw my daughter as a pillar of strength, determination, and passion, I was a ruin—broken, ramshackle, and ravaged by time, a sad, abandoned shell—but I was *still standing*.

It was time to do some serious repair work and heal.

Digging Deep

Ritual encourages focus, but it can also be comforting, so it was with a healing rite that I decided to begin to address the effect my past was having on my present. I say "begin," because maintaining, repairing, or rebuilding a life is a perpetual process. I couldn't erase my past; it would always be with me, always challenging me to move forward from it rather than be mastered by it. It's through these most intense moments, these moments of "getting it," that we learn our most valuable lessons.

The first thing I wanted to do was formally acknowledge what had happened to me and, at last, let it go. At the new moon (the perfect time to set the groundwork for a fresh perspective), I started by writing out all the details I could remember about that painful period of my life.

It was a slow and exhausting process. Thinking about and recording the details of what I'd gone through was like trying to break a massive boulder apart with a chisel. Eventually it would happen, but only

by tracing and tapping into the most vulnerable parts of the stone—
or, literally, me.

I let myself cry. A lot.

As much as it hurt to recall certain events, it was good to see it all
down on paper—and even better to see the ink run and blur when
tears hit the pages (amazing, the cleansing power of saltwater!). When
I finished, I read over what I'd written silently to myself, then sealed it
with a spell of spoken words:

> *These things happened.*
> *They hurt.*
> *I own them,*
> *But they do not own me.*
> *It is as I say,*
> *So mote it be.*

Then I made a little bonfire.

Cremating my memories didn't change the past, but it helped me say goodbye to the events and resulting feelings that had been weighing me down for too long. On a symbolic level, the process was purifying. I reserved some of the ash for the work to come, and cast the rest to the wind, an offering of gratitude to the universe: those experiences were part of the life my soul had chosen to live, and I had lived to tell the tale.

Tower of Power, Wall of Wonder

No matter how negative a situation may be, there is always something positive in it, even if it's small: a moment of peace, a kind word or smile from a stranger. I felt that knowing there had always been positive signs around me would make it easier to really let go of any lingering resentment I was holding on to. My intention was to build a new foundation of health and self-confidence from the positive aspects of those years—literally—with an altar.

I had ignored my own beauty for a long time, so it was important to me for my altar to be aesthetically pleasing in every way. For inspiration, I turned to Pagan artisan Carolina Gonzalez, who creates altars for spiritual services as part of her daily practice (http://caminodeyara .indiemade.com).

"Being an artist as well as a Witch makes every altar a complete creation, very much like a painting," Carolina told me. "Any surface can be the blank canvas, the elements used to create it are the colors, and the finished result is an accumulation of energy in a specific time and space frame. Just like a painting can soothe you, enlighten you, or make you dream, an altar does the same thing at a much deeper level, and can heal, restore, and provide for our spiritual needs. It is a transformative work at all levels, of self-exploration and connection; again, exactly the same process that being an artist requires."

If you want to try or adapt this ritual for yourself, I found that it's a good idea to make some preparations before you begin, so the work, which takes place over an extended period of time, can be seamless. You'll need:

- A pillar candle made from biodegradable material, such as beeswax or soy, so that any leftover wax can be returned to nature.

- A tool for carving your candle.

- Glitter in colors that correspond to your situation. I chose red and gold for confidence and success.

- Oil to dress your candle. I chose Van Van oil, as the positive, protective nature of this Hoodoo blend added yet another uplifting note to my purpose (plus it smells really good!).

- Pennies minted in the years of your life that require healing.

- Some ash from your writing bonfire.

- Herbs that have healing properties that correspond to your situation. Use your favorite herbal reference or, better yet, your intuition to choose what you will use. On building her altars, Carolina told me: "I draw mainly from the present and its energies. After I have chosen a purpose for the altar (for example, celebrating the full moon), I look around me and search for the elements that are filled with more energy at that specific time, such as seasonal plants, fruits, and symbols. My magic is strongly focused on local/bioregional elements, so the offerings and ornamentations come from my own garden or from the local farmers' market, as well as food cooked from scratch. I also incorporate stones, woods, bones, or other elements that I have wild-harvested myself."

My purpose was to release anger and pain, while at the same time focusing on the happy moments I knew were hiding in the corners of my memory. I wanted a combination of plants that would be aromatically uplifting and pretty to look at so that every aspect of the work would be focused on the positive. I chose lavender and lemon balm because I liked the scent of the potpourri, and the plants were readily available from my garden. I was right to follow my nose: both herbs soothe and promote peace, and lavender has antidepressant qualities.

- Post-it notes in bright, happy colors.

- Pens.

- Fabric and cord in colors that correspond to your situation. These will be used to hold any material that is left over once the ritual is complete. I chose yellow cloth with a sun pattern on it and gold cord—sunny yellow for the disposition I wanted to possess going forward, and gold, again, for success.

The central feature of my altar was a turquoise blue candle. Candles have always been an important part of my magic. I was raised Catholic, a faith where candles are a conduit for prayer and intercession. Blue is a peaceful, healing color, and the turquoise hue corresponds to the throat chakra, the energy center in the body that rules communication; I wanted to express my feelings honestly and clearly.

I carved my name in a heart on the top and bottom of the candle to symbolize that I surrounded myself with love and that this work began and ended with me. Then I dressed the candle with the oil and rubbed the glitter into the letters and hearts.

Next, I carved niches around the candle in a spiral from the top to the bottom. I tucked a penny into each niche so they formed a little winding staircase around the candle. Each penny represented one

troublesome year. The copper, being a conductor of energy, would channel the positive aspects of those years through the flame and light the way.

I filled a bowl with the herbs and some of the ash from my bonfire and nestled the candle inside it. Then I placed it on my empty altar with these words:

Wax and wane,
Joy and pain,
That's how it goes,
That's how life flows.
The wheel turns,
The candle burns.
Begin again
With the past as my friend.

The candle rose up from my altar like a tower. When I lit it, it became a beacon, and by its light, I would build a wall of strength.

Each "brick" in my wall was a neon-bright Post-it note on which I wrote a single positive encounter that occurred during my years of pain, including winning a contest, having an understanding teacher, and visiting relatives I loved. I placed the notes around the candle, leaving a small gap between each one until I'd formed a square. The chinks in the wall were made purposefully so that any lingering negativity would not be trapped inside. It was free to be released, with love.

As happy memories came back, I wrote them down and added layer after layer to the wall. The candle burned and the days slipped by. Recollections would sneak up on me, so I kept Post-it notes everywhere—in my desk, in my car, in my bag, next to my bed, and by the altar itself.

A few times, the candle went out and I had to fiddle with the wax. When this happened, I would look at the date on the penny that marked the level where things had gotten held up. I'd think about that year and try to recall what it was about that period that was particularly challenging. Then I'd focus on the positives that happened at that time—a family holiday, a special birthday present, reading a favorite book—then write them out and add them to the wall. The exercise made me realize that there had been more good in my life than I'd remembered.

It took about a month for the candle to burn out completely, but I kept the altar intact and added bricks to the wall until the next full moon, a time of fulfillment.

Time Capsule

The altars that Carolina Gonzalez creates are impermanent offerings assembled from consumable or reusable items. "My altars are impermanent because life is," she told me, "and just as life and nature flow in cycles, so do my altars." Carolina wastes nothing. Food is shared with friends and family, and plants are reused in incenses, herbal baths, and sachets. Like Carolina, I would waste nothing. Besides, the remnants of my altar still had work to do.

First, I dismantled the wall. I reviewed each brick before taping it into my journal so that I would have a record of the good aspects of my troubled times. As for my candle, all that was left of it was a mass of penny-studded wax that smelled faintly of lemons and was dusted with dried herbs, glitter, and ash. I would use these leftover elements of my altar to create a time capsule, a physical representation of the good memories I'd collected, a talisman to remind me of my strengths and my blessings.

I ground the remnants together with a mortar and pestle before wrapping them in the sun-patterned cloth. Then I knotted the cloth into a little bundle with the gold cord and a few magical words:

I give thanks for the past,
The good and the glad,
The joy and the sorrow,
The brave and the sad.
When times get tough,
To this I will hold:
To be happy and bright,
To be golden and bold.

Since performing the ritual, I've been confronted with situations that revived feelings that I'm sure are linked to my past. I'm convinced that the universe, like a good teacher, keeps handing us

opportunities—sometimes uncomfortable ones—that are meant to help us grow. My talisman has quietly done its work, reminding me to draw on my strengths as I continue to repair and rebuild. Some days are more challenging than others, but that is the nature of living in the midst of construction.

The day may come when I won't need my talisman–time capsule anymore. When it's time, I'll take it to a place of running water where I'll unwrap it, throw the remnants in, and watch them sink to the bottom or float away with a farewell and thank you. I will be another step closer to being completely healed. Until then, I'll keep it close and celebrate the life I have built.

Natalie Zaman *is a regular contributor to various Llewellyn annual publications. She is the co-author of the* Graven Images Oracle *deck (Galde Press) and writes the recurring feature "Wandering Witch" for* Witches & Pagans *magazine. Her work has also appeared in* FATE, Sage Woman, *and* newWitch *magazines. When she's not on the road, she's chasing free-range hens in her self-sufficient and Pagan-friendly back garden. Find Natalie online at http://nataliezaman.blogspot.com or at http://broomstix.blogspot.com, a collection of crafts, stories, ritual, and art she curates for Pagan families.*

Illustrator: Rik Olson

Leaping from Zeus's Head: How Athena Helps Combat Negative Thinking

Tiffany Lazic

It is dark. The lights are off. The mysterious moon is high in the sky. There is no glow from television, computer, or even phone. Melatonin should be working its slumbering magic. The sandman should have visited by now. Fluffy sheep have proven to be of no use whatsoever. As you lie stretched out on your place of rest and restoration under the blanket of the quiet night, the thoughts that have been playing at a low thrum all day rise to a twisted cacophony. You feel like the embodiment of the nine of swords card in the Tarot. You sit up in bed, head in hands, overcome with despair. Again.

An estimated seventy million people in the United States suffer from insomnia. Though eating habits and physical discomfort can impact the ability to fall asleep, worry is a major contributing factor. When the bustle of the day recedes, concerns about health, finances, relationships, jobs, children, and countless other aspects of life can easily come to the fore, making much-yearned-for sleep a distant hope.

Worry is negative visualization. When we worry, we create frightening scenarios in our heads. We imagine the worst possible outcomes and tell ourselves that these will happen. How we worry about different areas of our lives provides insight into a far more important element. Worrying shows us what we believe about ourselves to be true. Action follows emotion, which follows belief. What we believe to be true creates an emotional response within us. Emotions inform our choices, either consciously or unconsciously. The actions we undertake are always in response to the feelings that flow through us, positively or negatively. Uplifting emotions such as courage, hope, love, passion, and joy are not an issue. They are wonderfully supportive and provide vital energy to carry us through many a challenge. It is emotions such as fear, anger, resentment, despair, and bitterness that can jam our circuits, leading to negative thinking and possibly depression.

> **Worry is negative visualization. When we worry, we create frightening scenarios in our heads. We imagine the worst possible outcomes and tell ourselves that these will happen.**

Grabbing hold of one of the swords that hangs so precariously over your head, you find it represents the rumors regarding company downsizing. Night after night, instead of falling into a blissful, healthy, body-revitalizing sleep, you lie awake scaring yourself with scenes of being called in to human resources, of clearing out your office, of not being able to find other work, of not being able to pay the mortgage, of having to cut out your children's extracurricular activities and lessons. The music track of these terrifying scenes consists of this almost-indiscernible chant: "You are powerless. You are helpless. You are ineffective." Anxiety knots your stomach, and you feel helpless, powerless, and ineffective. You continue to jab at yourself with an endless loop of thoughts that you feel powerless to address or change. There is nothing you can do. It is inevitable. Everything is going to fall apart. Each morning, you arise a little more exhausted and a little more discouraged.

The goddess Athena holds dominion over wisdom and just war. She is the guide in justice, inspiration, strategy, and the development of skill. She is the patroness of heroes and the champion of heroic endeavors. Known primarily as Zeus's daughter, she does have a mother—Metis, the Titan goddess of advice, planning, and cunning. Prophecy held that Zeus would be overthrown by the son he had with Metis. As this outcome was simply not conceivable to Zeus, he decided to thwart the prophecy by removing Metis from the equation. In true Greek god–like form, he swallowed Metis whole. But he did not realize that Metis was already pregnant. Not long after Metis settled in his stomach (from where she continued to give him counsel), Zeus developed an excruciating headache. One can imagine that, with head in hands, Zeus did not manage to catch much sleep either. When it became too much to bear, he asked to be struck by a labrys (the Minoan double-sided ax), a task undertaken (most tales say) by Hephaestus, the blacksmith god. What a surprise, then, when out from the wound made in Zeus's head stepped Athena, fully grown and fully armed.

There is wisdom to be gleaned from the painful thoughts in our heads. When the inner negative thought cycle becomes too much to bear and we finally turn into the pain instead of trying to ignore or avoid it, what gift of wisdom and prudence steps forth? What tools does Athena offer that can help us cleave negativity open, providing new avenues of opportunity?

Owls and Athena go hand in hand. Owls have long been associated with wisdom, but in particular the wisdom that comes from being able to see in the dark. Almost all owls are nocturnal, and their ability to find tiny creatures to nourish them in the blackest of nights is remarkable, particularly given that owls do not rely on echolocation. They actually do see in the dark. Owls are far-sighted and have the ability to turn their heads 270 degrees, due to the fourteen neck vertebrae they have (compared with the seven found in humans). We become stuck when we can only see things from one perspective, and feeling stuck always leads to a negative thought cycle. Wisdom comes from being able to see in unlikely places, with the expanse of long-range understanding and the flexibility of many angles.

Snakes are intertwined with Athena with their presence on her aegis, her shield of protection. There are two versions of Athena's aegis. One variation of her story presents that it was made for her by Hephaestus of highly polished bronze and was used by Perseus to slay the snake-haired Gorgon Medusa (who actually became snake-headed as a punishment by Athena herself). The other variation holds that it was crafted by Athena out of the skin of a monster she had slain. In both versions, the aegis is emblazoned with snakes. In later myths, Athena fastens Medusa's head to the front of the aegis so her enemies may be turned to stone. Snakes enjoy a rather convoluted reputation in myth, oftentimes representing the entrance to a dangerous path (as in the snakes that make up Medusa's hair). But snakes are also our guides to wisdom through transformation. They are associated with regeneration and awakening. Being able to shed old patterns, limiting beliefs, and inner critical messages opens us to live from a place of authenticity and empowerment.

Less prominent perhaps is Athena's association with the olive tree. When both Poseidon and Athena vied for patronage of a beloved city, they each bestowed a gift upon the citizens to win favor. Poseidon struck the ground with his trident, revealing a spring. But with Poseidon being god of the sea, the spring water was salty and of little use and benefit. Athena gifted the city with the olive tree, which provided wood, oil, and food. It was Athena's gift that was accepted, and thus the city of Athens was named in her honor. Not only does the olive tree offer the practical elements necessary for basic survival, but its branches have long symbolized peace—the invitation to release conflict and confrontation.

Owl, olive, snake, and aegis. Each one is a powerful tool for combating negative thinking.

Owl, olive, snake, and aegis. Each one is a powerful tool for combating negative thinking.

Clarity comes with the light of day, but deep wisdom comes in the depth of night. It is human nature to want to avoid the dark. But if we allow ourselves to sink into the dark and peer at the shadowy corners of our minds, what will we find? What lies beneath the worrying scenarios that play out in our minds? Owl gives us the sight to look beyond the initial vision that swims before our eyes. From the heights of the sky, Owl helps us pierce the thoughts to see the truth beneath. Snake teaches us to shed the skin that has become too constricting. Snake's perspective low on the earth guides us to be grounded and practical in our approach to transforming our circumstances. The olive tree brings peace of mind and opens us to become clear about what really matters. And the aegis offers us protection, particularly from external detractors who might criticize, belittle, or shame us.

Grabbing hold of the sword that hangs so precariously over the head once again, you turn it over in your hands, observing it from all angles. You are aware of all the feelings it brings up in you—the anxiety, the hopelessness, the bitterness. You hear the taunting inner chant that urges you to feel small and incapable. With Athena by your side, you call upon Owl's far-reaching wisdom and Snake's practical resilience. Beyond the vision of the human resources discussion, you see options for actively addressing the potential situation: a proactive meeting with a recruitment firm, a résumé filled with your skills and experience, a negotiation that results in a settlement package, or even the reassurance that it is only rumors that are circulating and, if downsizing does in fact happen, you will be well prepared. You hear the underlying chant of "You are capable; you are effective; you are valuable" that wraps around you like a protective aegis, knowing that, no matter what comes your way, you have the power to make the best decisions for yourself in every moment. It doesn't matter if the company determines that you are no longer a necessary part, or if economists herald doom and gloom. Both of those may very well happen, but your truth is that you are valuable and you alone are capable of finding the niche where your value is appreciated. The outside situation may be uncertain and changes may very well be in the air, but you know you have

what it takes to provide for your own survival, and within your own mind, there is peace.

Athena was born out of fear and pain. But in spite of the elements contributing to Athena's appearance in the world, not only did Zeus claim her as his daughter, but she became his favorite. In times of chaos and uncertainty, Athena's discernment is a gift and a balm. When you find yourself feeling overwhelmed, dismayed, or depressed, seize the shield and release your concerns to Athena. Allow her wise guidance to come to you on owl wings and snakey slither. And feel the peace grow within you like a hardy, resilient olive tree.

Bright-eyed Athena, stately and proud,
Guide me to my highest truth.
Guide me to my greatest strength.
Guide me to prudence in thought and action.
Wise goddess of discernment,
Connect me ever to the source of my wisdom within,
And awaken in me the fire of courage and the flame of empowerment.

Tiffany Lazic *is a Spiritual Psychotherapist with over sixteen years' experience in individual, couples, and group therapy. As the owner of the Hive and Grove Centre for Holistic Wellness, she created and teaches two self-development programs, Patterns of Conscious Living and Spiritual Language of the Divine, and also teaches in the Transformational Arts College of Spiritual and Holistic Training's Spiritual Directorship and Divine Connections Training Programs. An international presenter and keynote speaker, Tiffany has conducted workshops for many conferences and organizations in Canada and the UK, including the 2013 Energy Psychology Conference. She is a member of the Sisterhood of Avalon, where she serves on the Board of Trustees, and in the Avalonian Thealogical Seminary. Tiffany is the author of* The Great Work: Self-Knowledge and Healing Through the Wheel of the Year *(Llewellyn Publication, 2015).*

Illustrator: Jennifer Hewitson

Cerridwen: Meeting the Witch Goddess

Kristoffer Hughes

When the chairs come to be judged, mine will be the best of them. This is my song, and my cauldron, these are my rules. In the court of Don I am called the knowledgeable one.

—from "The Chair of Cerridwen," Book of Taliesin

Autumn leaves rise in a vortex of wind as silver-lined clouds billow across an ebony sky. The clouds part to reveal a sickle-sharp moon, and her waxing face illuminates the landscape below. Beneath the lunar light, a solitary Witch rises from her knees, her skin glistening with fragrant oils. Her arms lift to the skies as words of power fall from her lips. She stands, she summons, she calls to the Witch Goddess:

> O Goddess supreme, your Awen be mine!
> Awaken, arise, your wisdom to shine.
> Cerridwen, wise one, keeper of seeds,
> Arise, I beseech thee, witness my deeds!
> O Goddess supreme, by Awen divine,
> Awaken, arise, your magic be mine!

The land sighs to the call of the Witch as she and bark, leaf, and tree, berry and stone and bone, dance together in union. The Witch and the land become as one, and the Witch Goddess arises from the memory of ancestors, from the whispers of nature and the power of the Witch. And in that moment, there is connection. The chasm of time and distance collapses, and what was then becomes what is now. Time and place are suspended in the exquisite dance of Witch and Witch Goddess.

Further words of power fall from the Witch's lips, and her hands, alive with magic, charge the herbs and powders that she casts into the cauldron's belly. Her spell is chanted, her intention projected, and swimming with her spirit she senses the ancient power of the Witch Goddess, who whispers her secrets into the core of her being.

. . . .

One could be forgiven to imagine the above to be a scene from a movie, or maybe a page from a novel. Surely it paints a farfetched picture of a Witch in the throes of her magic? On the contrary, the scene is one that I am intimately familiar with, of a rite that conjures more than just imagination, but the power of the Witch Goddess Cerridwen.

Cerridwen is a Celtic goddess who is mentioned several times in the manuscripts of the Celtic people of Wales, notably the Book of Taliesin, the Black Book of Carmarthen, and the Ystoria Taliesin. The latter recounts the initiatory allegorical tale of the birth of the bard/prophet/magician Taliesin. In a nutshell, Cerridwen takes to brewing a cauldron of Awen, an ancient Welsh name for the underlying energetic force of the universe, to imbue her son with all the wisdom and knowledge of all the worlds. The Awen can only realistically be expressed through our creativity, something that Cerridwen hoped would compensate for her son's dreadful ugliness. So she took to her craft and set a cauldron to boil for a year and a day, into which herbs of the land would be cast. The cauldron and its fire were tended to by a blind man and a young boy called Gwion Bach.

Alas, at the end of the year and a day, three drops of pure Awen leaped from the cauldron and landed on Gwion Bach's thumb instead. His eyes burned with magic, and he knew all things past and all things yet to come. In her fury, Cerridwen gave chase; in the guise of various animals, she chased Gwion through the three realms of land, water, and sky. Finally, in the guise of a black hen, she swallowed Gwion into her belly, only to give birth to him nine moons later. The child she had vowed to kill for cheating her son of the Awen was so beautiful, her heart broke at the sight of him. So she placed him within a skin coracle and set him afloat on a river. Four decades later on the night of Samhain, the coracle was found in a salmon weir. Within it lay a child with a glowing brow, and he was named Taliesin, meaning "he with the radiant brow."

Taliesin is remarkable in that he represents pure connection; in essence, he is the universe singing in praise of itself. In the Ystoria Taliesin, he says: "I received the Awen from the Cauldron of Cerridwen. And I was moved through the entire universe. And I shall remain until the end of time upon the face of the earth. And no one will know what my flesh is, whether meat or fish. I was nine months in the womb of the Witch Cerridwen. I was formerly Gwion Bach, but now I am Taliesin." (Translated by the author from NLW 5276D Manuscript, National Library of Wales.)

Taliesin is the epitome of the connected initiate; he knows all things, has been all things, and is the embodiment of magic. And yet, the conduit for the initiatory journey is Cerridwen. The mystery teachings of Taliesin and Cerridwen relay an important message: we, too, can be equally connected.

We are informed in the old legends that Cerridwen was learned in the ways of the Craft, specifically magic, enchantment, and divination. To align with her in the path of Witchcraft and magic today is to step into a stream of enchantment that reaches back into the distant past, to access a storehouse of wisdom that swims in the currents of tradition.

Cerridwen, in typical Celtic manner, has three defined functions, each of which relates to one of the three realms of land, water (sea), and sky. In her land aspect, she is the Mother; her sky aspect is the expressive, creative, and transformative qualities of Witch; and as Goddess, she represents the singularity and omnipresent nature of the sea. Each function acts as an ally to the Witch who connects to her. In her role as Mother, Cerridwen presents to us a deeply human aspect; vulnerable, flawed, and yet immensely caring and loving, she teaches us that it's okay to be human, to make mistakes. As the great Mother, Cerridwen offers spiritual nourishment and sustenance, a guiding hand through the forest of magic and an unconditional love that only a mother can possess. As an accomplished and learned Witch, she is the great teacher. Capable and committed to her craft, she is the perfect magical companion during training, practice, or study. Finally, in her guise as Goddess, she bridges the chasm between the physical and deep mystery, a conduit between the human Witch and the lofty realms of the divine. Through all these guises, Cerridwen teaches us a valuable lesson: we are not alone. We have at the reach of relationship a vast cauldron of magical allies to assist, sustain, and teach us, perhaps none as powerful and effective for the Witch as Cerridwen.

Witches do not glean all their knowledge entirely from books; they also access and make use of subtle natural powers and forces that accentuate and heighten their abilities. Encounters with the Witch Goddess on a purely academic basis, where one attempts to glean meaning only from the written word, pale in comparison to the rapturous relationship one can achieve in a visionary sense. Encounters with Cerridwen are incredibly powerful, and aligning yourself to her can initiate a lifelong relationship that will transform your craft.

> **Encounters with Cerridwen are incredibly powerful, and aligning yourself to her can initiate a lifelong relationship that will transform your craft.**

What I offer here is a tried and tested method of connecting to Cerridwen, one that is useful for any Witch, regardless of rank or experience. You may be an aspiring Witch, immersed in study and training, in which case Cerridwen will offer you a guiding hand through the dappled groves of Witchcraft. You may be an experienced Witch who seeks to immerse herself deeper into the mysteries of the cauldron that Cerridwen protects, in which case Cerridwen in her guise as Witch and Goddess is an invaluable ally.

To initiate contact with Cerridwen, immerse yourself in the following visualization and ritual.

Calling the Witch Goddess

Create a space that can be made sacred in whatever way you are accustomed, and ensure you will not be disturbed for an hour. Perform this ceremony late at night with only candlelight to illuminate the space. Incense heavy in resins such as pine or copal will add to the atmosphere.

In the center of your space, place a small cauldron or other similar vessel, and sit down comfortably before it. Around the cauldron, arrange three smaller vessels to represent the powers of land, sea, and sky. Position the land vessel to the left of the cauldron, and place within it an item that represents your human life, such as a photograph of yourself, a lock of your hair, or a poppet made in your semblance. Position the vessel that represents sky to the right of the central cauldron, and within it deposit an item that represents your magical persona. This could be a necklace, a sacred object or tool, or perhaps a poem, story, song, or piece of art that represents your creativity. Finally, position the sea vessel behind the central cauldron, and place within it a stone that has come from a beach or riverbed or has been submerged in natural water.

Ensure you are comfortable, then close your eyes and take a deep breath with the land beneath you. Take another deep breath and pull down the power of sky into your lungs. Now cast your awareness out and take a breath with the sea, rivers, and lakes of your land. Imagine the ground beneath you dissolving; carpet, tile, or board vanish, and you find yourself upright in mid-air, a heavy mist beneath you. What would it feel like to float, to be held by air? A sudden wind tears at the mist, which parts to reveal a moonlit landscape carved by ice. A long, narrow lake edged by mountains and woodland greets your eyes—this is Lake Bala in the mountains of Wales, Cerridwen's home.

Breathe deeply and descend. A wooden pontoon, formed of rough wooden planks, floats in the center of the lake. Upon it sits a cauldron

surrounded by three vessels just like the ones that occupy your sacred space in the physical world. Your feet touch wood. The pontoon wobbles slightly, and the waves lapping at its side sing the song of water. The sickle-sharp moon hangs like a lamp at the head of the valley, and a long silver corridor of light glows toward your point in the center of the lake. With hands outstretched, the following words tremble from your lips:

> O Goddess supreme, your Awen be mine!
> Awaken, arise, your wisdom to shine.
> Cerridwen, wise one, keeper of seeds,
> Arise, I beseech thee, witness my deeds!
> O Goddess supreme, by Awen divine,
> Awaken, arise, your magic be mine!

The silver corridor swells just ahead of you, and the form of Cerridwen rises slowly from the glistening water. Long dark hair covers her features, and her fluid-like dress is made of water and moonlight. She sweeps toward the pontoon on which you stand and glides out of the water. Her naked feet slap  the boards as she joins you. Separated only by the cauldron, you are confronted by the Witch Goddess herself.

Once more, your lips tremble as words of power fall from them:

O Goddess supreme, your Awen be mine!
Awaken, arise, your wisdom to shine.
Cerridwen, wise one, keeper of seeds,
Arise, I beseech thee, witness my deeds!
O Goddess supreme, by Awen divine,
Awaken, arise, your magic be mine!

Her hair sweeps aside to reveal her face, and your heart skips a beat at her countenance. Cast your spirit toward her, and tell her your name. Speak to the image of the Witch Goddess, and begin your exquisite connection and relationship to Cerridwen. Bask in her presence for as long as is comfortable. When it feels right, allow her image to collapse into water; her form loses its shape and name and returns to the lake from whence she came. Your feet lift from the boards and your arms extend skyward. As you lift, the mists return, obscuring your vision of Lake Bala. The familiarity of your own physical space returns.

Breathe deeply with the land beneath you and reach out to your left, grasping whatever item you placed in the land vessel. Hold it in your left hand, consider what it represents, and place it directly into the central cauldron as an offering. Then say:

O Goddess supreme, your Awen be mine!
To my human form let your wisdom shine.

Now reach to your right and take the item you placed in the sky vessel. Consider its qualities and place it directly into the central cauldron. Then say:

Cerridwen, wise one, keeper of seeds,
To my spirit arise, come witness my deeds.

Finally, reach forward and take the stone that you placed in the sea vessel. As you do so, know the mystery: there is but one sea; all rivers and lakes lose their names and forms as they enter the sea, but their essence remains. This emulates the nature of the gods and goddesses: they are everywhere and nowhere simultaneously. Place the stone in the central cauldron and say:

O Goddess supreme, by Awen divine,
My soul doth awaken, your magic be mine!

The cauldron represents the mysteries of Cerridwen; she is its primary keeper and guardian. Hover both your hands above the central cauldron and sense your offerings being absorbed into the otherworld, into the lap of Cerridwen. Sit in quiet contemplation for a while.

What do your offerings represent? What do they say about your life? Speak to the Witch Goddess. Tell her your story. Tell her why you have come to meet her. When the time feels right, return to your normal state of awareness and close the ritual in whatever way you are accustomed. Place the cauldron and its contents in a place that has significance to you—an altar perhaps, or a bookshelf. Then each night, as your mind turns toward sleep, return to the wooden pontoon at Lake Bala and call to the Witch Goddess. Deepen your connection to her, and allow her message of wisdom, enchantment, and magic to filter through your dreams and inspire your waking life.

Whenever you need Cerridwen's help, simply take to your cauldron or invoke its image and utter the words of magic:

O Goddess supreme, your Awen be mine!
Awaken, arise, your wisdom to shine.
Cerridwen, wise one, keeper of seeds,
Arise, I beseech thee, witness my deeds!
O Goddess supreme, by Awen divine,
Awaken, arise, your magic be mine!

Kristoffer Hughes *is the author of* From the Cauldron Born: Exploring the Magic of Welsh Legend and Lore *and* The Book of Celtic Magic: Transformative Teachings from the Cauldron of Awen. *He is head of the Anglesey Druid Order and a Mount Haemus Scholar. He lives on the Island of Anglesey, just off the coast of North Wales.*

Illustrator: Tim Foley

The Divine Masculine for Women

Diana Rajchel

Entire festivals and libraries of books revolve around Goddess work. Pagans venerate their goddesses, often to make up for the complete absence of the feminine divine in previous religious lives. On the other hand, work that helps women approach the God on new, healthy, non-patriarchal terms happens only when individual women create that path for themselves. Without this work, the wounded relationship between the divine masculine and living women remains, bloody and infected.

The first step in this healing is by far the most difficult. Culture is oxygen. Our culture is patriarchal. Oxygen and patriarchy are both invisible, and a Goddess religion in the midst may itself struggle with what it does not realize it cannot see.

The male gods we invoke live in a dimension that we do not know, and that no one in living priesthood has witnessed. This masculine isn't just an absent father, an errant spouse, or a drop-in lover. This god makes half the world go round.

To begin the work of connecting to and rethinking the God in relationship to women, we must look at the common roles connected to the masculine divine.

The Cosmic Force

While not as popularly recognized as Cupid, his younger equivalent, Eros was one of the oldest gods in the Hellenic pantheon. He emerged from the chaos of the universe itself, embodying the complementary urges of creation and freedom. Invocation of this god might apply to creative arts, social change, or even scientific innovation. All things to be begin in Eros, so identifying that energy can help you identify the spark of something.

EXERCISE

Go stargazing. Lie flat on your back and stare up at the sky, imagining that your entire being has merged with the cosmos. As you relax into this imagining, listen or feel for a pulse, almost like a heartbeat. Breathe in time with that rhythm. As you do, send out a mental signal seeking the flavor of male energy within that pulse. Is all of it male? Is it masculine, as you know masculine? Hold on to this sensation for as long as you can, then let go gently, becoming aware of the earth beneath you, the sounds around you, and the temperature of the air.

The Sun and Moon

Life would not exist without the sun and could not survive and live in balance without the regulating forces of the moon. Not only does Greek sun god Apollo have the all-revealing light of truth, but he chose a woman, the Oracle of Delphi, to bring his voice to the mortal world.

Exercise

Over the course of one day, observe the sunrise and sunset. If you can, step outside and feel the sun at its zenith. As you observe, feel light soaking into you at sunrise. Imagine this time as the start of a day-long conversation with the intelligence within sunlight. Ask it, at each point in the day, if it feels male or female. Ask it why it thinks of itself as that particular gender at that time of day.

Thoth, the Egyptian god of the moon, presents an interesting challenge to those who perceive the moon as exclusively feminine. Thoth is a regulator to other gods, which means he knows how to apply the silent, feminine force of justice, Maat. This alignment suggests that real justice requires participation of both masculine and feminine energies.

EXERCISE

Under a full moon, pour out a libation of mead or honey. Extend an invocation to Thoth:

> Hail to Thoth,
> keeper of scrolls—
> Ibis god, keeper of the scales,
> keeper of secrets,
> Let us converse and know each other this night.
> Help me to know your lunar ways!

Pay attention to your physical responses. Does your skin feel cold, tingly, or hot? Do you feel pressure from a presence filling up space nearby? Observe images that flash in your mind. Look for specifics in that energy to identify as specifically male. Ask Thoth how he sees himself, even if it feels like a silly question.

When you have finished, thank Thoth, and tell him you must depart.

On the next night, invoke a lunar goddess, such as Diana. Pay attention to the difference in physical responses and sense of presence. Offer a libation, and then explore the energy, looking for what you sense as distinctly female. When finished, thank the goddess invoked.

Journal your experiences and compare them.

The Thundering Rain

Reconstructionists may cringe at the thought, but it may be time to reframe Zeus for a world in which women have more rights than they did in ancient Athens. Rather than think of Zeus as the abusive, cheating spouse, consider him as the god who gives zaps when needed. His thunderbolt appears on the Tower card in the Tarot. Zeus also birthed the being who corrected his relationship with women. His son Dionysus emerged from his thigh (after Zeus unwillingly killed his mother) and, while known as a god of the vine, ruled thunderstorms. Dionysus's cult members, the maenads, were oppressed women and men whom his worship freed from societal injustice. While the maenads are often depicted as mythical, violent, supernatural creatures, there was a cult of real human women and male slaves who participated in the orgiastic rites. Dancing in the first thunderstorm of spring became an offering to Dionysus.

EXERCISE

Sit by a window during a thunderstorm and watch the rain until it stops. Pay attention to how the sound of thunder feels inside your body. Look for male energy in that. Pay attention to your own feelings about the storm and the energy within you, and pay attention to any emotional traces you feel from the storm.

For those of you living in an environment unconducive to thunderstorms, try performing an invocation of Zeus. Put together a small votive offering, such as a printed-out image of Zeus or a small clay tablet with the word "Zeus" inscribed on it, to bury when finished.

Here is one invocation you might use:

> Thundering god of the mountains, I invoke you. Be gentle with me,
> O Lord. I seek to understand the nature of your energy.

From there, sit down and visualize Zeus sitting in front of you. You may wish to pour a glass of wine, one for you and one for him, and talk about what masculinity means to the likes of Zeus.

When finished, speak your farewells and thanks.

At the next storm, invoke Dionysus. Dance while singing or shouting his name. If you cannot dance, speak an invocation such as this:

> Hail, god of the vine, sprung from Zeus's thigh, man borne of man,
> champion of women, I invoke you!

Sit where you can watch the rain and engage in a conversation with Dionysus. Ask him how he sees masculinity. You may find yourself questioning your impressions. For the space of the ritual, simply accept the odd images, thoughts, smells, and sounds that may come to you. When finished, pour a libation of wine or grape juice and thank Dionysus for his insights.

The Hunter

The hunter archetype can apply to—or switch—genders. The best known divine hunter, Artemis, was female, though she often took male hunters as compatriots. She, like Apollo, often had her gendered energy offset by representatives of the opposite gender on Earth, such as Adonis and Orion.

In Celtic lore, Herne represents the hunter. He may also serve as an avatar of Cernunnos, the Horned God depicted on the Gundestrup cauldron. Herne represents the male mysteries, the experiences of men unknowable to women. (Whether or not these mysteries are nontransferable is in increasing doubt, given the rising number of people able to get sexual reassignment.)

EXERCISE

Find a quiet area in nature and be still for as long as you can. In this time of stillness, feel all the energy of nature around you, and in your imagination, seek out the thread of masculine energy. When you finish, thank the nature around you. Once a day for the next month, recall that stillness, wherever you are. After each session, write down any insights you get into masculine energy—and underline those that defy stereotypes regarding what men "should" be.

The Wild God

The god Pan represents the forces of nature that farmers cannot control. Another horned deity—this one with the feet and horns of a goat instead of a stag—Pan represents the essence of nature's id. His representation in Tom Robbins's novel *Jitterbug Perfume* speaks best to the nature of this god and to his relationship with women: he is the irresistible pull of nature itself, the voice of the body free from the voice of society. As an extension of that nature, he can also be something terrible and frightening—not out of malice, but simply as an expression of nature.

EXERCISE

Steep a tea of juniper and cedar wood. Go outdoors and pour the tea onto the ground as a libation while praying to Pan. For example, say:

Be gentle with me, wild god.
Teach me about your dance,
about your energy,
about what male means in your world.
Be mindful of my mortality
as you show me your ways.
So mote it be!

Then sit outside and listen to all the sounds around you. Pay close attention to the responses of your body—what you feel and where—during this work. When you have finished this meditation, pour out a second libation, of wine this time, and thank Pan for the gentle lesson.

The Farmer

The tale of the Egyptian god Osiris is one of a leader better suited to domestic than military policy. Osiris, as the god who was killed by political enemies and then rose again, spoke to literal fertility, yes, but also to the absolute necessity of sacrifice in leadership—and provided the underpinnings of myths where women must be preserved and protected to ensure continuity of life and culture. This again leads to the question: Why this division? Men have the same capacity as women to relay information and culture. In the Egyptian tale, it was Isis, the female partner, who had political and inter-tribal (the ancient equivalent of international) savvy.

EXERCISE

Take an apple seed and go outside on a warm day. Place the seed on your palm and hold it up to the sun, with your fingers extended. Concentrate on the heat gathering on the coat of the seed. Think about the sensations the seed might feel under the sun, and then imagine the sun's sensation as it touches the seed. Search, in that heated space where light and seed meet, for a sense of masculinity. Once you attain this sense, plant the seed and give thanks to the sun, the earth, and the seed.

The King

While actual invocation of King Arthur seems relatively rare, as he is usually passed over in favor of Herne, the tale of the divine king marks leadership passing from women, as represented by Morgaine, to men, as represented by Arthur. Those who resonate with the Mists of Avalon see these legends as the final transition into patriarchy. Yet Arthur himself, while living in a restrictive society, is not wholly concerned with reassignment of power. Throughout this tale and several variations of the legends about his knights, women, while cast in increasing shadows and mystery, are significant in major decisions. It is made clear that women want (and should have) sovereignty, though it seems that the world considered it a bad time to give them that. When Arthur dies, women receive his body and look after his burial in a way that parallels both the Pagan divine king and the tale of Christ and his resurrection. While not much

discussed, it appears that Arthur himself represents a willing ally to women. In the time of his legends, he may not have had the ability to change the status of women, the implication being that the women themselves have that power and have chosen not to use it, or have forgotten that they have that power.

Read a series of myths and history about kings and queens. Choose two or three eras, or two or three countries, to compare and contrast. As you read, make a chart: What decisions were made and what calamities happened under the kings in your reading? What decisions were made and what calamities happened under the queens? What unique leadership decisions were especially bad? What leadership decisions were good? Compare the nature of the decisions to the gender of the leader—are there common threads? If you read across eras, did the typical decisions alter, or switch, genders at any point?

The Sacrifice

The one role beyond fertilization that the male aspect of divinity fills is that of sacrifice. It is always the king, or the sacrificial volunteer, who dies for the land. In these stories, the masculine divine doesn't relinquish his power so much as turn it over to his female partner or his heir. Along with this death comes the compensation of reincarnation. Why men bear this weight—while women bear the weight of eternity—is one of the greater spiritual mysteries.

Read as many different versions of the same sacrificial god myth as you can find. Examples of these gods include Osiris, Dionysus, King Arthur, and John Barleycorn. After each myth, meditate on the story, running it through your mind as you examine it for elements of distinct masculine energy. Make note of how different versions of the same tale can alter your perspective.

In addition to altering these concepts of the male divine, it may help to set aside or reframe the old beliefs in male-female polarity. Men can provide projective or receptive magic; women can do so equally. The physical gender of the person makes no difference, except in cases where the ability to fertilize or be fertilized is significant. Many on the Goddess path see the Goddess as the Great Mother and the God as the Great Father. Together, they form the gigantic pillars of all that we know of the universe, the mothers and fathers of all. When we come to these paths, however, we often carry the wounds of our microcosmic relationships. Therefore, we see the Goddess and God as our parents—and then many of us run into trouble, more often with the father than with the mother, when negative parental relationships color our view of our own faith. The father-daughter relationship has received the most negative attention and backstory since the Goddess movements began.

So how do women create a listening and speaking role for the divine masculine in their own practice? What place does he have in a theology that allows for magic?

For a woman of the twenty-first-century Goddess religions, the only real obstruction to having a profound relationship with a male divinity is inaction. Not all women want or will benefit from inclusion of male energy in their practice, but for those who resonate with gendered duotheism, any effort to build that second, balancing relationship can provide the benefit of an enriched worldview.

Diana Rajchel *is a third degree Wiccan priestess in the Shadowmoon tradition. She fills Pagan infrastructure gaps with services to people of all spiritualties relating to life, death, birth, and peace of mind. Author of* Divorcing a Real Witch *and books on Mabon and Samhain, she has written on topics relating to Paganism and the occult since 1999. Rajchel is also an experienced tarot reader, has a lively interest in how American folk magic like hoodoo can apply to modern life, and is fascinated by modern urbanism and how magical lifestyles fit with it. At present, she lives in the San Francisco Bay Area with her partner.*

Illustrator: Kathleen Edwards

The Inward Bridge: Massage and the Mind-Body Connection

Elizabeth Barrette

Bodywork covers a wide range of techniques used to soothe the mind and body. In general, though, massage heals through the application of healthy touch. Some of it is about manipulating the body to fix things that aren't working properly. Some of it is more about making people relax and feel good. All of it helps bring the mind and body into concert.

The Need for Touch

Primates in general, and human beings in particular, need healthy touch. This isn't a high-level enrichment need. It's a fundamental survival need. Babies and children who do not get enough loving touch will not thrive, and tend to die. Those who survive suffer from stunted development physically, mentally, and emotionally. Adults who are lonely have higher health risks than those with strong social connections. People kept in solitary  confinement also develop mental health problems from the isolation. People need each other, and they need skin contact, in order to stay healthy.

Gentle touch reassures us that we are loved and wanted. Different cultures have different ways of meeting this need. European friends hug and kiss cheeks upon greeting each other. African-American folks sometimes wear their hair in elaborate braids, and enjoy the hours it takes for someone to put their hair up. Little girls in many cultures play hand-clapping games together. Massage, like hair braiding, can be a kind of social grooming. Closely related is helping each other put on sunscreen. All of these things fulfill a similar desire in different ways.

People connect with each other through touch. We shake hands, bump fists, or nudge each other for guidance. Closer friends and family members hug and cuddle. Touch reminds us that we are not alone, that people are there for us and we are there for them.

In a magical context, skin contact enhances many abilities, such as empathy and healing. If you need more energy movement, try increasing the surface area where skin meets skin. Touch through fabric is less effective but still works somewhat. Remember that silk and most synthetics tend to insulate against subtle energies, which can be an advantage or a disadvantage.

It gets more complicated for people who find touch to be abrasive rather than comforting. Some are touch-averse for physical reasons, such as sensory processing disorder (SPD). Others are touch-averse due to psychological reasons, as abuse survivors often are. But they may still suffer the effects of not getting enough touch. Massage is one way to deal with those challenges. Many people with SPD find deep pressure soothing even if a light touch is aggravating. With survivors, it's often the opposite; they may benefit from light, careful contact and especially if they are the ones initiating it.

Physical Aspects of Bodywork

Massage produces a wide range of specific effects, and overall it is an adaptogenic treatment: it tends to improve negative conditions without also reducing positive ones, helping the mind and body heal themselves. This makes it useful for many different complaints, especially in complex situations with several problems interacting.

Skin contact releases endorphins. These reduce pain and deliver pleasant feelings. This is especially beneficial for chronic conditions that can't be fixed. Massage can also increase serotonin and dopamine levels, thus helping to protect against depression. At the same time, it decreases cortisol, a stress chemical that impairs the immune system.

Broad strokes improve circulation, both of blood and lymph fluid. This addresses a variety of conditions that cause poor blood flow, and also aids the immune system. Furthermore, broad strokes stimulate the nervous system. They boost neural communication between body and brain and improve muscle tone. They even have an antihistamine effect—usually noticed as a reduction in irritation from bug bites or allergies after you've gotten a massage for some other reason. This type of massage is also used for emotional care.

Deeper strokes manipulate tissues and improve flexibility and motion. This helps with damaged skin (scar tissue, stretch marks) and

muscles (cramps, overwork). It can also aid tight or achy joints by loosening the connective tissue. Most bodywork aimed at physical therapy for treating specific conditions will include strokes of this type. However, some people with other conditions also respond well to this—autistic people who find light touch uncomfortable often enjoy deep pressure.

Bodywork in general stimulates the elimination of toxins and bodily wastes. In particular, it encourages skin excretion through sweat, a key reason for following massage with a warm bath or shower to open the pores. This is part of how it removes things like cortisol and histamines. It flushes out all the bad stuff but doesn't cause your body to dump valuable nutrients.

Massage can relieve or at least improve many physical conditions, such as arthritis, asthma, carpal tunnel syndrome, digestive disorders, fatigue, headaches, high blood pressure, insomnia, muscle cramps, neurological pain, and sport injuries. For back problems, it can reduce pain and improve mobility. Athletes use bodywork to prepare for sporting events and also to soothe the body after a hard workout. In family care, massage helps provide shorter, easier labor for mothers and promotes weight gain for infants.

Mental Aspects of Bodywork

Massage affects the mind through the body. It flushes out cortisol and histamines, both of which are associated with emotional as well as physical discomfort. This helps reduce irritation, anger, anxiety, and depression. Massage promotes serotonin, dopamine, and endorphins, all of which correlate with positive emotions. So this encourages feelings of peace, relaxation, and happiness. You can use magic, including empathy, to support these effects.

Just being touched feels good to most people. The gentle contact and compassionate attention from another person helps create a sense of connection and meaning. For this reason, massage is sometimes used in coordination with counseling to solve internal or interpersonal issues.

More seriously, many people tend to "store" tension or memories in their muscle tissue. This causes cramps that can significantly impair function. Some types of deep-tissue bodywork are specifically designed to address these problems by releasing the tension, which not only eases the muscular strain but also makes it more feasible to work through the underlying emotional issues. If you are doing energy work along with physical bodywork, then this tendency grows stronger. However, you may stumble upon buried memories during any kind of bodywork—most massage providers have seen a recipient inexplicably burst into tears due to a suddenly recurring memory. Sometimes just being in a safe place brings things out.

For survivors of trauma, massage can create or restore a sense of security. Some people have never learned, or have forgotten, what it feels like to be safe. Bodywork requires building a rapport between provider and recipient. When done right, it allows for the experience of vulnerability in a secure environment, which helps alleviate hyperarousal and apprehension.

Bodywork influences brainwaves and thus the state of consciousness. A long, slow massage promotes relaxation. This happens because the brain produces more delta waves, those that correlate with deep sleep or meditation. It's why people tend to zone out or even fall asleep on the massage table. Conversely, a shorter and more energetic massage has an invigorating effect on consciousness. This is often done in a massage chair at business events. That brings up alertness, the alpha waves of focused concentration. These waves are slower and smoother than the quick beta waves of ordinary consciousness. The alpha state is ideal for creativity and decision making.

Overall, massage improves positive mental and emotional factors such as concentration, energy, self-compassion, and sleep. When you treat yourself well, you feel better. Massage can also reduce problems such as abuse aftermath, anger management issues, anxiety, attachment disorders, depression, stress, touch starvation, and trust issues.

Uniting Mind and Body

Problems in the mind can affect the body, and physical complaints can create mental issues. In either case, the mind and the body tend to slip out of tune with each other. Massage offers a unique opportunity to synchronize the mind and the body, because it influences both of them. When the different aspects of yourself are in harmony with each other, then you will feel better.

Magical practitioners tend to maintain a psychic shield around themselves, usually in layers. For massage or energy work, openness produces better results. However, you don't want random crud floating in to bother you either. An effective approach is for provider and receiver to lower their outer shields (keeping the inner ones for privacy unless they're close friends or family) and shield the room around both. This allows personal energy to flow more freely in response to the skin contact between the individuals.

Centering is another important step that facilitates effective bodywork. Here the energy flow in question lies within your body. Imag-

ine your energy body as a stack of rings. When the rings are out of alignment, they constrict the flow of energy through your middle; the process of centering brings them into a neat stack and maximizes the throughput. The long, full-body strokes during a massage help stimulate subtle currents in the body so the power moves in productive ways—much the same as it stimulates the movement of blood and lymph fluids.

Grounding connects you to an outside energy source, most often the earth, though it can be another element or higher power. An invigorating massage instills energy; grounding ensures that any excess energy drains away to avoid causing nervousness. A relaxing massage releases tension; grounding helps stabilize that process and prevents you from losing too much energy. It is vital for the provider to have good grounding skills, because doing bodywork and energy work solely with your own power is exhausting. Having a connection to an outside source ensures that you don't deplete yourself while working.

Along with your physical body, you have an energy body. It has layers and subdivisions, much as your material body has skin and organs. Working with the energy body helps connect your mind with your flesh.

The chakra system is one way of describing that organization of energy. Chakras are little balls or pools of life force. The main ones are centered along the spine, from your tailbone to the top of your skull. This is one reason why just a back rub can make your whole self feel better: pressing the back from base to top will stimulate the chakras in order, making the energy flow from one to another. The energy is supposed to cycle through your body in a way similar to water in a recirculating fountain. Massage helps balance out the chakras by strengthening weak ones and tapping off excess energy from overcharged ones. This brings your mind and body into tune. At the end of a session, many providers will place a hand over the neck (throat chakra) or back (heart chakra) and tailbone (sacral chakra) even if they don't know about energy centers. It helps balance and ground the power.

The meridian system is another way of mapping the energy body. Meridians are lines that run through the major organs, with points along them that can produce useful effects if stimulated. These run along a course similar to major nerves in the physical body. Meridians are used in acupuncture, acupressure, and some other alternative health care schools. In bodywork, you may find "tender spots" along the merdians that relate to persistent complaints, based on energy blockages. Massage can be helpful as a broad and gentle way of smoothing out tangled energy, especially for someone who can't tolerate more focused treatment of hypersensitive areas.

Sometimes people find it useful to employ tools or supplies to aid in achieving the mind-body balance. Aromatherapy uses scent to improve mood and energy. It can relax or invigorate, depending on which substances are chosen. Aromatherapy combines beautifully with bodywork because you can just put a few drops of essential oil into the carrier oil (such as grapeseed or apricot kernel) used as massage oil. Scent activates memory, a primal connection between mind and body.

Stones are also popular. A chakra-balancing set contains a rainbow of gemstones, from red to violet, that help tune each of the chakras in order. However, gems aren't the only stones with power. Basalt is a plain rock used in hot stone massage because it holds heat very well. The dark rocks also aid grounding, and the weight anchors the mind in the body—beneficial for anyone who tends to space out or who has trouble connecting with their body.

. . . .

For magical practitioners, it is vital to keep the mind and body in balance. That provides a secure foundation for both spellcraft and spirituality. Massage addresses mind and body together and brings them into harmony, making it especially useful. Try it—you'll be glad you did!

Elizabeth Barrette *has been involved with the Pagan community for more than twenty-three years. She served as managing editor of* PanGaia *for eight years and dean of studies at the Grey School of Wizardry for four years. Her book* Composing Magic: How to Create Magical Spells, Rituals, Blessings, Chants, and Prayers *explains how to combine writing and spirituality. She enjoys magical crafts, historical religions, and gardening for wildlife. Visit her blog,* The Wordsmith's Forge (http://ysabetwordsmith.livejournal.com), *or her website,* PenUltimate Productions (http://penultimateproductions.weebly.com).

Illustrator: Bri Hermanson

The Lunar Calendar

September 2015 to December 2016

SEPTEMBER

S	M	T	W	T	F	S
		1	2	3	4	5
6	7	8	9	10	11	12
13	14	15	16	17	18	19
20	21	22	23	24	25	26
27	28	29	30			

OCTOBER

S	M	T	W	T	F	S
				1	2	3
4	5	6	7	8	9	10
11	12	13	14	15	16	17
18	19	20	21	22	23	24
25	26	27	28	29	30	31

NOVEMBER

S	M	T	W	T	F	S
1	2	3	4	5	6	7
8	9	10	11	12	13	14
15	16	17	18	19	20	21
22	23	24	25	26	27	28
29	30					

DECEMBER

S	M	T	W	T	F	S
		1	2	3	4	5
6	7	8	9	10	11	12
13	14	15	16	17	18	19
20	21	22	23	24	25	26
27	28	29	30	31		

2016

JANUARY

S	M	T	W	T	F	S
					1	2
3	4	5	6	7	8	9
10	11	12	13	14	15	16
17	18	19	20	21	22	23
24	25	26	27	28	29	30
31						

FEBRUARY

S	M	T	W	T	F	S
	1	2	3	4	5	6
7	8	9	10	11	12	13
14	15	16	17	18	19	20
21	22	23	24	25	26	27
28	29					

MARCH

S	M	T	W	T	F	S
		1	2	3	4	5
6	7	8	9	10	11	12
13	14	15	16	17	18	19
20	21	22	23	24	25	26
27	28	29	30	31		

APRIL

S	M	T	W	T	F	S
					1	2
3	4	5	6	7	8	9
10	11	12	13	14	15	16
17	18	19	20	21	22	23
24	25	26	27	28	29	30

MAY

S	M	T	W	T	F	S
1	2	3	4	5	6	7
8	9	10	11	12	13	14
15	16	17	18	19	20	21
22	23	24	25	26	27	28
29	30	31				

JUNE

S	M	T	W	T	F	S
			1	2	3	4
5	6	7	8	9	10	11
12	13	14	15	16	17	18
19	20	21	22	23	24	25
26	27	28	29	30		

JULY

S	M	T	W	T	F	S
					1	2
3	4	5	6	7	8	9
10	11	12	13	14	15	16
17	18	19	20	21	22	23
24	25	26	27	28	29	30
31						

AUGUST

S	M	T	W	T	F	S
	1	2	3	4	5	6
7	8	9	10	11	12	13
14	15	16	17	18	19	20
21	22	23	24	25	26	27
28	29	30	31			

SEPTEMBER

S	M	T	W	T	F	S
				1	2	3
4	5	6	7	8	9	10
11	12	13	14	15	16	17
18	19	20	21	22	23	24
25	26	27	28	29	30	

OCTOBER

S	M	T	W	T	F	S
						1
2	3	4	5	6	7	8
9	10	11	12	13	14	15
16	17	18	19	20	21	22
23	24	25	26	27	28	29
30	31					

NOVEMBER

S	M	T	W	T	F	S
		1	2	3	4	5
6	7	8	9	10	11	12
13	14	15	16	17	18	19
20	21	22	23	24	25	26
27	28	29	30			

DECEMBER

S	M	T	W	T	F	S
				1	2	3
4	5	6	7	8	9	10
11	12	13	14	15	16	17
18	19	20	21	22	23	24
25	26	27	28	29	30	31

2015
SEPTEMBER

SU	M	TU	W	TH	F	SA
		1	2	3	4	5
6	7 Labor Day	8	9	10	11	12
13 ● Solar Eclipse, New Moon 2:41 am	14	15	16	17	18	19
20	21	22	23 Mabon/ Fall Equinox	24	25	26
27 ☺ Lunar Eclipse, Harvest Moon 10:51 pm	28	29	30			

Times are in Eastern Time.

2015
OCTOBER

SU	M	TU	W	TH	F	SA
				1	2	3
4	5	6	7	8	9	10
11	12 ● New Moon 8:06 pm Columbus Day (observed)	13	14	15	16	17
18	19	20	21	22	23	24
25	26	27 ☺ Blood Moon 8:05 am	28	29	30	31 Samhain/ Halloween

Times are in Eastern Time.

2015
NOVEMBER

SU	M	TU	W	TH	F	SA
1 All Saints' Day/ DST ends 2 am	2	3 Election Day (general)	4	5	6	7
8	9	10	11 ● New Moon 12:47 pm Veterans Day	12	13	14
15	16	17	18	19	20	21
22	23	24	25 ☺ Mourning Moon, 5:44 pm	26 Thanksgiving Day	27	28
29	30					

Times are in Eastern Time.

SU	M	TU	W	TH	F	SA
		1	2	3	4	5
6	7	8	9	10	11 ● New Moon 5:29 am	12
13	14	15	16	17	18	19
20	21 Yule/ Winter Solstice	22	23	24 Christmas Eve	25 ☺ Long Nights Moon, 6:12 am Christmas Day	26
27	28	29	30	31 New Year's Eve		

Times are in Eastern Time.

2016
JANUARY

SU	M	TU	W	TH	F	SA
					1 *New Year's Day*	2
3	4	5	6	7	8	9 ● New Moon 8:31 pm
10	11	12	13	14	15	16
17	18 *Martin Luther King, Jr. Day*	19	20	21	22	23 ☺ Cold Moon 8:46 pm
24	25	26	27	28	29	30
31						

Times are in Eastern Time.

2016
FEBRUARY

SU	M	TU	W	TH	F	SA
	1	2	3	4	5	6
		Imbolc/ Groundhog Day				
7	8 ●	9	10	11	12	13
	New Moon 9:39 am					
14	15	16	17	18	19	20
	Presidents' Day (observed)					
21	22 ☺	23	24	25	26	27
	Quickening Moon, 1:20 pm					
28	29					

Times are in Eastern Time.

2016
MARCH

SU	M	TU	W	TH	F	SA
		1	2	3	4	5
6	7	8 ● Solar Eclipse, New Moon 8:54 pm	9	10	11	12
13 DST *begins 2 am*	14	15	16	17 St. Patrick's Day	18	19
20 Ostara/ Spring Equinox	21	22	23 ☺ Lunar Eclipse, Storm Moon 8:01 am	24	25	26
27	28	29	30	31		

Times are in Eastern Time.

2016
APRIL

SU	M	TU	W	TH	F	SA
					I	2
					All Fools' Day	
3	4	5	6	7 ●	8	9
				New Moon 7:24 am		
10	11	12	13	14	15	16
17	18	19	20	21	22 ☺	23
					Wind Moon 1:24 am Earth Day	
24	25	26	27	28	29	30

Times are in Eastern Time.

2016
MAY

SU	M	TU	W	TH	F	SA
1	2	3	4	5	6 ●	7
Beltane					New Moon 3:30 pm	
8	9	10	11	12	13	14
Mother's Day						
15	16	17	18	19	20	21 ☻
						Flower Moon 5:14 pm
22	23	24	25	26	27	28
29	30	31				
	Memorial Day (observed)					

Times are in Eastern Time.

2016
JUNE

SU	M	TU	W	TH	F	SA
			1	2	3	4 ● New Moon 11:00 pm
5	6	7	8	9	10	11
12	13	14 Flag Day	15	16	17	18
19 Father's Day	20 ☺ Strong Sun Moon 7:02 am Litha/ Summer Solstice	21	22	23	24	25
26	27	28	29	30		

Times are in Eastern Time.

2016
JULY

SU	M	TU	W	TH	F	SA
					1	2
3	4 ● New Moon 7:01 am Independence Day	5	6	7	8	9
10	11	12	13	14	15	16
17	18	19 ☺ Blessing Moon 6:57 pm	20	21	22	23
24	25	26	27	28	29	30
31						

Times are in Eastern Time.

2016
AUGUST

SU	M	TU	W	TH	F	SA
	1	2 ●	3	4	5	6
	Lammas	New Moon 4:45 pm				
7	8	9	10	11	12	13
14	15	16	17	18 ☺	19	20
				Corn Moon 5:27 am		
21	22	23	24	25	26	27
28	29	30	31			

Times are in Eastern Time.

2016
SEPTEMBER

SU	M	TU	W	TH	F	SA
				I ● Solar Eclipse, New Moon 5:03 am	2	3
4	5 Labor Day	6	7	8	9	10
II	12	13	14	15	16 ☺ Lunar Eclipse, Harvest Moon 3:05 pm	17
18	19	20	21	22 Mabon/ Fall Equinox	23	24
25	26	27	28	29	30 ● New Moon 8:11 pm	

Times are in Eastern Time.

2016
OCTOBER

SU	M	TU	W	TH	F	SA
						1
2	3	4	5	6	7	8
9	10	11	12	13	14	15
16 ☺ Blood Moon 12:23 am	17	18	19	20	21	22
23	24	25	26	27	28	29
30 ● New Moon 1:38 pm	31 Samhain/ Halloween					

Times are in Eastern Time.

2016
NOVEMBER

SU	M	TU	W	TH	F	SA
		1 All Saints' Day	2	3	4	5
6 DST *ends 2 am*	7	8 Election Day *(general)*	9	10	11	12
13	14 😌 Mourning Moon, 8:52 am	15	16	17	18	19
20	21	22	23	24 *Thanksgiving Day*	25	26
27	28	29 ● New Moon 7:18 am	30			

Times are in Eastern Time.

2016
DECEMBER

SU	M	TU	W	TH	F	SA
				1	2	3
4	5	6	7	8	9	10
11	12	13 ☺ Long Nights Moon, 7:06 pm	14	15	16	17
18	19	20	21 *Yule/ Winter Solstice*	22	23	24 *Christmas Eve*
25 *Christmas Day*	26	27	28	29 ● New Moon 1:53 am	30	31 *New Year's Eve*

Times are in Eastern Time.